Parsleys, Fennels, and Queen Anne's Lace

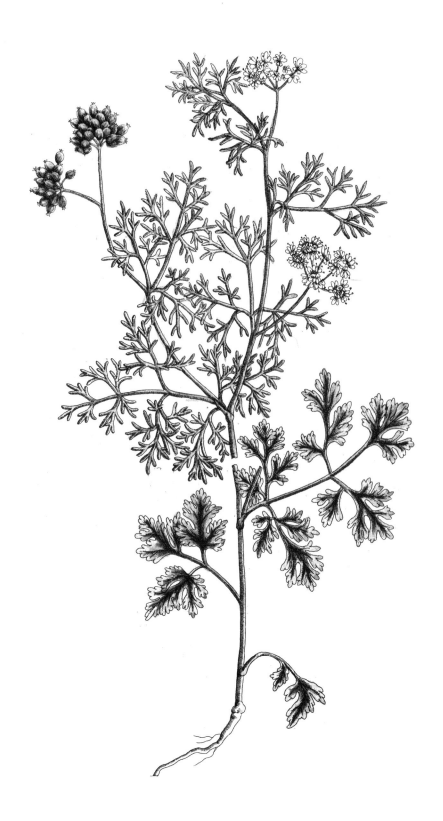

Parsleys, Fennels, and Queen Anne's Lace

❧

HERBS AND ORNAMENTALS FROM
THE UMBEL FAMILY

❧

Barbara Perry Lawton

TIMBER PRESS

Frontispiece: *Coriandrum* from Elizabeth Blackwell's *A Curious Herbal*
(1737). Missouri Botanical Garden Sturtevant Pre-Linnaean Collection.

Published in 2007 by
Timber Press, Inc.
The Haseltine Building
133 S.W. Second Avenue, Suite 450
Portland, Oregon 97204-3527, U.S.A.
www.timberpress.com
For contact information regarding editorial, marketing, sales, and
distribution in the United Kingdom, see www.timberpress.co.uk.

Printed in China

Library of Congress Cataloging-in-Publication Data
Lawton, Barbara Perry.
  Parsleys, fennels, and Queen Anne's lace : herbs and ornamentals from
the umbel family / Barbara Perry Lawton.
     p. cm.
  Includes bibliographical references and index.
  ISBN-13: 978-0-88192-822-8
  1. Umbelliferae. 2. Parsley. 3. Fennel. 4. Carrots. I. Title.
  SB351.U54L39 2007
  635.9'33849—dc22
                                                    2006013502
A catalog record for this book is also available from the British Library.

*Once again, I thank Bill and Cindy and their families
for their interest and encouragement*

Contents

Preface   9

CHAPTER 1 Umbels in History and Lore   13
CHAPTER 2 Medicinal and Poisonous Umbels   26
CHAPTER 3 Edible Umbels   38
CHAPTER 4 Ornamental Umbels   47
CHAPTER 5 Umbels in the Wild   58
CHAPTER 6 Pests and Diseases   75
CHAPTER 7 Botany of Umbels   81
CHAPTER 8 A Catalog of Umbels, from *Aciphylla* to *Zizia*   87

Finding Information and Plants   143
U.S. Department of Agriculture
    Hardiness Zones   144
Glossary   145
Further Reading   149
Index of Plant Names   152

Color plates follow page 48

Preface

IMAGINE! Here are popular vegetables, herbs, and spices in the same family as the world's most poisonous plants. Plants that have played a role in the deaths of many ordinary people and at least one major historical figure are closely related to those prized for their culinary and medicinal virtues. And in centuries past, people believed some of these herbs had magical qualities that would repel evil: hang dill over your doorway to keep the devil away.

As you will discover in chapter 1, there are surprises to be found in this fascinating plant group. Since learning the details of Socrates' deadly tea of poison hemlock, I have developed such a respect for that plant that I observe the gigantic clumps that appear along a railroad track near me only from a healthy distance. And since I learned the story of English horticulturist Ellen Willmott's sowing of seeds (fruitlets, actually, as we will discover) of the pale and ghostly sea holly, when I see the plants in a garden bed, I envision Miss Willmott surreptitiously strewing the fruitlets as she strolled through others' gardens.

The umbel family (or parsley family), Apiaceae or Umbelliferae, is a large one. Exact numbers vary depending on the authority, but according to Mark Griffiths (1994) there are some 418 genera and about 3100 species. Since the taxonomy is not yet carved in stone—indeed, the botanists I have talked to agree that there's a long way to go in understanding the relationships of the genera and species—there is much disagreement as to how many plants constitute this family.

As I researched this book, I was astonished to discover the

breadth and depth of the parsley family. Now that I've peeked in the door, I have learned that the umbels are in many ways more challenging than the plants of the mint family, which I wrote about in *Mints* (Timber Press 2002).

We're all somewhat familiar with members of the Apiaceae through our gardens and grocery stores. We know carrots, celery, parsley, dill, and fennel. More enlightened gardeners and cooks may also be acquainted with angelica, chervil, caraway, and the umbelliferous spices.

Who is not familiar with Queen Anne's lace, the handsome, white-flowered volunteer of the fields of summer and fall? Yet I'll bet you didn't know that Queen Anne's lace is the ancestor of our cultivated carrot. The next time you see a mature plant, pull it up by the roots to see the pale taproot that horticulturists developed into the fat, sweet carrots of our contemporary diet.

I am drawn to the Apiaceae not only for the graceful, feathery growth of the plants, which adds a lightness to any garden design, but also for the rich traditions with which the family has been involved over the centuries in its relationship to humans. The fragrances and flavors of the culinary umbellifers are familiar to anyone who appreciates fine food. The history of these plants in medicine is less well known but is traceable through the old herbals, such as those I have studied at the Missouri Botanical Garden Library.

As I researched the umbellifers, I found scads of species I'd never heard of, many of which are interesting prospects for the garden. I even found plants growing in my own region, the Midwest, that I had been unaware of. For instance, at a winter meeting of the Missouri Native Plant Society, there was a wild chervil on display in a collection of plants that remain green throughout the cold months. I have one of the small, pressed specimens on my bulletin board.

Because many of the umbels are useful herbs, I think it's important to realize that the word *herb* is used in several ways. In the strictest sense of the word, an herb is a plant with distinctly useful attributes, such as dill or fennel, which are used in the culinary arts. In another sense, an herb is a plant with medicinal, house-hold, or aromatic uses. Finally, in the larger botanical sense, an herb is a soft-textured plant that dies back to the ground in temperate regions when the cold seasons arrive. And, of course, an herbal is a book dedicated to describing plants that are useful to mankind.

If you don't already love the umbellifers, I hope perhaps this book will cultivate a new appreciation for this fascinating family, from the elegant, aromatic herbs and vegetables to the most vile of poisonous plants.

Acknowledgments

A tip of the hat and my sincere appreciation to the many people who were so helpful in researching this book. Once again, thanks to Peter Raven, director of the Missouri Botanical Garden, for putting me in touch with botanist experts on the umbelliferous plants of the world. Mark Watson, an expert in umbellifer systematics, who conducts floristic research on China and the Himalaya, was particularly helpful in helping me fathom the taxonomic morass of the Apiaceae. My very special thanks to Pete Lowry, taxonomic botanist and expert on the Apiaceae and closely related Araliaceae, who not only suggested a couple of excellent resources but also helped make my botanical chapter more accurate and readable. I especially appreciate his reading and editing of chapter 8.

Much appreciation to both Kay and George Yatskievych, who were kind enough to hold my hand and suggest directions for my research when I occasionally painted myself into a corner. Special appreciation goes to Kay for loaning me a slide of harbinger of spring (*Erigenia bulbosa*) after I had missed its blooming time by a few days. Naturalist James Trager of the Shaw Nature Reserve sleuthed out several native umbels, an invaluable help to me, since the reserve covers hundreds of acres.

I very much appreciate the loan of some handsome images of ornamental members of the parsley family from Jelitto Staudensamen GmbH of Jelitto Perennial Seeds in Germany. I also appreciate the kind assistance of Jelitto's American representative, Allen Bush.

Thanks to Cindy Gilberg, who, in addition to being my daughter, has been a great help in getting photographs and suggesting umbels to include. Thanks, too, to Harlan Hamernik of Bluebird Nursery, who provided information about some wonderful ornamental umbels that are quite new to the American gardening scene. The people at Timber Press were also great to work with, always ready to offer a leg up when needed. Without the help of these and others, I couldn't possibly have written this book.

Once again I have been able to bring some of the treasures of the Missouri Botanical Garden rare books collection to my readers. My special appreciation goes to the garden's library, its director, Doug Holland, and the library's very helpful staff. The library is known worldwide for its valuable books, including the Sturtevant Pre-Linnaean Collection. The books in this fabulous collection were published from 1474 to 1753. They were printed prior to the publication of *Species Plantarum* (1753), written by the father of binomial nomenclature and scientific classification, Carl Linnaeus. The collection is named after E. Lewis Sturtevant, an agriculturist and botanist who generously donated his collection of 463 volumes to the garden in 1892. The Sturtevant Pre-Linnaean Collection has grown since then and now includes more than 1100 volumes. I have selected several images from these rare books to help illustrate the Apiaceae and its many genera and species.

CHAPTER 1

Umbels in History and Lore

THE PARSLEY FAMILY was one of the first plant families to be described as such. It was called *Narthekodes* by Greek philosopher and scientist Theophrastus (371–287 BCE), and later became the first family to be scientifically systematized in the modern sense. The family was a project of Scottish scientist Robert Morison (1620–1683), who published his *Plantarum Umbelliferarum Distributio Nova* in 1672, many years before Linnaeus arrived on the botanical scene.

The history of Apiaceae and its relationship to mankind is a rich and varied one. This chapter provides a glimpse into what is undoubtedly a fascinating subject, but there is much more to learn. The history of the old herbals, for example, is a lengthy and complex subject in and of itself. Should you find that this introduction piques your interest, I strongly encourage you to pursue more information in libraries or on the Web.

Ancient Records

The earliest records of these plants are vague, fogged over by the centuries. Before there was written language, oral traditions passed knowledge of herbs and herbal usage from generation to generation. We do know that archeologists have found traces of ancient plants, primarily large quantities of pollen, among human remains in a 60,000-year-old burial site in Iraq (Mesopotamia). In 1960, archeologists discovered the burial site of the Neanderthal man in Shanidar Cave, northern Iraq. Upon study, the pollen proved to be from at least eight different medicinal plants. Although some nay-sayers insist the pollen grains were incidental to the site, many others believe the man was given a ritual burial that included flowers covering his body. If this is the case, perhaps the plants were for his use in the world beyond death. Were there umbels in those plant remains from so many tens of thousands of years ago? We can't know for sure, but it is highly likely, since many of the useful umbels of ancient times, including dill, fennel, angelica, parsley, and coriander, were commonly found growing in regions around the Mediterranean, Middle East, and other parts of Eurasia.

By 3500 BCE, the ancient Egyptians are said to have turned from magic to herbs for the treatment of sickness. Illustrations found on Egyptian tomb walls dating back to about 2000 BCE indicate a familiarity with herbs. For instance, references to dill have been found on artifacts of early Egypt (as well as in ancient Greece).

For some of the earliest herbal references, we must also look to China. The great emperor Shěn-nung (c. 3000 BCE), known as the Divine Healer, may be mythical or may truly have been a part of Chinese history. It is said that he ate 365 medicinal plants during his lifetime, so many that he eventually turned green and died of plant toxicity overdose. Although the earliest reliable historical source of plant references is in a Chinese dictionary that dates only to about 350 CE, Shěn-nung's knowledge of medicinal plants appears to have been handed down through the centuries by herbalists and healers. A catalog of herbs that lists 252 medicines derived from plants has been attributed to Shěn-nung but was actually written sometime between 25 and 221 CE.

Huang Di (2697–2595 BCE), the so-called Yellow Emperor, is considered the founding father of Chinese medicine. Like Shěn-nung, he may be mythical or may have some basis in truth. He is credited with China's first book on medicine, *Nei Jing* (The Yellow Emperor's Canon of Medicine). This book, made around 1000 BCE, many hundreds of years after Huang Di's lifetime, is supposedly based on Huang Di's conversations about medical diagnoses and treatments with Qi Bo, a famous Chinese physician.

Old Herbals

The history of herbs is best exemplified by the old herbals. These illustrated books about plants were usually written by physicians and served as manuals for selecting and preparing remedies for various complaints and diseases.

Theophrastus is credited with writing the first herbal, *De Historia Plantarum* (A History of Plants), produced around 300 BCE. It includes scientific descriptions of some 500 herbs. He also wrote *De Causis Plantarum* (About the Reasons of Vegetable Growth), with sections on herbaceous plants, vegetables, and herbs. An important early botanist of the Western world, Theophrastus was a pupil of Aristotle and his successor as head of the Lyceum. Aristotle bequeathed both his library and his unpublished works to Theophrastus, who continued working on them. Theophrastus was also in charge of the first botanical garden.

In the first century CE, Pliny the Elder, also an early Greek, wrote *Historia Naturalis* (Natural History), which consists of thirty-seven volumes and describes the medicinal uses of plants. He originated the doctrine of signatures, which held that plants with characteristics similar to certain ailments could be used to treat those conditions. For instance, plants with red sap could be used to treat blood disorders.

Another herbal from the first century is *De Materia Medica* by Pedanius Dioscorides. This is probably the most influential herbal of all time. It was popular well into the sixteenth century and was reproduced in some thirty-five editions in Latin and Greek. In it, Dioscorides describes 600 or so herbs and their medicinal virtues, stressing the importance of paying attention to the proven effects of these plants. Many of the herbs described remain in use today.

Pre-Linnaean Herbals

Among the rare books at the Missouri Botanical Garden is the Sturtevant Pre-Linnaean Collection, which covers the period from

1474 to 1753. The story of herbs and their usage, including the um-bels, is beautifully illustrated and described in these books. Images from several of them are reproduced in this book.

Peter Schöffer's *Herbarius*, printed in Mainz, Germany, in 1485, is the oldest printed and illustrated herbal of the garden's collec-tion. Though the artist is unknown, the woodcuts, printed by hand and painted with watercolor, have obviously been copied from the works of ancient physicians, especially Dioscorides.

Otto Brunfels' *Herbarum Vivae Eicones*, printed in 1530 in Stras-bourg, represents a giant step forward, as the artist, Hans Weiditz, based his drawings on the plants themselves rather than creating a stylized copy of ancient artwork. From a design point of view, the illustrations also blend well with the printed word.

Leonhard Fuchs' *De Historia Stirpium*, printed in Basel, Switzer-land, in 1542, represents yet another step forward in botanical art. The artists who worked on this herbal observed the plants they were drawing but also combined the features of several plants to create somewhat stylized versions rather than exact representa-tions. In the mid-1500s, William Turner produced the first scien-tifically oriented English herbal and illustrated it with some 400 beautiful woodcuts, mostly reproduced from the artwork in Fuchs' earlier herbal.

John Gerard, the famous Elizabethan herbalist, published *The Herball* in 1597, a tome that has been reproduced in recent times. I own a copy of the reproduction and often refer to it for its delight-ful illustrations and entertaining (and often still valid) references to the medicinal attributes of plants from all over the world.

Gerard's Old English is pretty catchy once you get the gist of it—the letter *f* for *s* probably causes the most confusion. Here is a typical example, in this case a description of coriander (I have sub-stituted *s* for *f* to make it a bit easier to understand):

The first or common kind of Coriander is a very stinking herbe, smelling like the stinking worm called in Latin *Cimex*: it hath a round stalke full of branches, two foot long. The leaves that grow lowest, and spring first, are almost like the leaves of Chervill or Parsley, but those which come forth afterward, and grow upon the stalks, are more jagged, almost like the leaves of Fumitorie, though a great deale smaller, tenderer, and more jagged. The floures are white, and do grow in round tassels like unto dill. The seed is round, hollow within, and of a pleasant sent and savour when it is drie. The root is hard, and of a wooddie substance, which dieth when the fruit is ripe, and soweth itself from yeare to yeare, whereby it mightily increaseth.

The 1633 edition of *The Herball*, "very much enlarged and amended" by Thomas Johnson, includes about fifty parsley family species with their illustrations. However, you would be hard put to match those umbels with today's umbels, since so many of the names and classifications have changed over the centuries.

My favorite herbalist has come to be Elizabeth Blackwell (1700–1758), née Blachrie, the artist and engraver for the beautiful plates of *A Curious Herbal*. We owe the existence of this handsome herbal to her ill-advised marriage to a man often described as a handsome rascal. Elizabeth Blachrie was the daughter of a successful merchant in Aberdeen, Scotland. As a young woman she studied art, an education that turned out to be most fortunate. Against the wishes of her family, she secretly married her cousin, Alexander Blackwell, an Aberdeen physician.

When Alexander's medical credentials were questioned, the couple fled to London, where Alexander joined a publishing company. When he opened his own printing house, it was soon discovered that he had not served the required apprenticeship, nor did he follow trade rules. Heavy fines resulted, forcing him to close his shop. That combined with his excessive spending habits soon exhausted Elizabeth's dowry and put Alexander into debtors' prison.

With a young daughter to support and no income, Elizabeth soon grew desperate. After hearing that a new herbal was needed to provide up-to-date descriptions of New World plants, she decided that with her art background she could illustrate such a book. Elizabeth had little botanical knowledge but thought that Alexander, with his background in medicine and science, could supply the text. She would take the completed illustrations to her jailed husband, and he would supply plant descriptions as well as accepted plant names, not only in Latin but also in Italian, Spanish, Dutch, and German.

Many of the plants that she would draw were located at London's Chelsea Physic Garden, and at the suggestion of Chelsea's curator, she relocated to lodgings nearby. There she drew the plants, engraved the copper plates that would be used to print the herbal, and hand-painted the printed illustrations. Although Elizabeth was never considered to be in the top rank of botanical illustrators, her work was praised by physicians, surgeons, and apothecaries, who had badly needed an updated herbal. The Royal College of Physicians also gave her a commendation, a great distinction for a woman to have earned at that time.

When income from *A Curious Herbal* had bought Alexander's freedom, you'd think he would have learned his lesson, but unfortunately he soon accumulated more debt. Eventually the Blackwells were forced to sell some of the rights to the herbal.

After Alexander failed in several more business ventures, he convinced Elizabeth that he should move to Sweden. There he practiced medicine and tried his luck at farming, and eventually the king appointed him court physician. Alexander's natural bent soon prevailed, however, and he became involved in an undercover scheme to revise the Swedish line of succession to the throne. Not surprisingly, the king and his men discovered the plot, arrested him, and condemned him to death by hanging. And Elizabeth? She, poor thing, continued to share her book royalties with Alexander until his death. And he never sent for his family to join him in Sweden.

Later, between 1757 and 1773, *A Curious Herbal* was reissued in Nuremberg in a revised and enlarged format. The elegant images of umbels reproduced in this book are from that edition.

Religious Texts

The importance and common use of umbelliferous herbs in the Middle East during the years before Christ is apparent in the Torah. Coriander (*Coriandrum sativum*) is referenced a number of times, for example, as in Exodus 16:31: "And the house of Israel called the name Manna: and it was like coriander seed, white; and the taste of it was like wafers made with honey." Parsley (*Petroselinum crispum*), though not mentioned specifically, was abundant in the Mediterranean region and was used at Passover as a symbol of a new beginning, since it was among the first herbs to appear in spring. In Song of Solomon 5:13, the female speaker rhapsodizes, "His cheeks are as a bed of spices, as banks of sweet herbs. His lips are like lilies dropping liquid myrrh." It is not clear whether the myrrh she refers to is the umbelliferous herb known as sweet cicely (*Myrrhis odorata*) or rather the valuable fragrant resin that comes from a small Mediterranean tree. (The latter is the myrrh given to the infant Jesus Christ by one of the Magi.)

The New Testament continues the herbal traditions: "Woe to you, scribes and Pharisees, hypocrites! For ye tithe mint and anise [most scholars translate this as dill] and cummin, and have left undone the weightier matters of the law, justice, and mercy, and faith" (Matthew 23:23).

General references to herbs also appear in the Koran, as in sura 2.61: "'Moses,' you said, 'we will no longer be patient with one type of food. Call on your Lord to bring forth for us some of the produce of the earth, green herbs and cucumbers, corn, lentils and onions.'" Sura 22, entitled "The Pilgrimage," includes the following sentence: "And ye see the earth parched, and when we send down water on it, it stirs and swells, and brings forth herbs of every beauteous kind." There is also mention of aromatic herbs in sura 55.12, which surely would have had to include some of the well-known umbels such as caraway, dill, and fennel. Again, although these are not specific mentions of umbels, deductively we know that they must have been included simply because of the region and the other knowledge we have of herbal usage in early times.

The Death of Socrates

Socrates (470–399 BCE) will always be associated with the most poisonous of all parsley family plants, poison hemlock (*Conium maculatum*). All parts of the plant contain an oily yellow sap that is highly toxic, but the most poisonous parts are the foliage, roots, and unripe fruit.

After getting out of the army, and without any regular employment, Socrates usually spent most of his time in the agora (marketplace) at the center of Athens. Poor by his own choice, he wore shabby clothes and went barefoot throughout the year. He was an ugly man, overweight, with a snub nose and eyes that bulged. An oracle had told him that he was the wisest man in all of Athens. He wandered the streets of the city asking metaphysical questions of the reputedly wise and in doing so discovered not only their ignorance but also his own wisdom in admitting his ignorance.

Just imagine living in that time in Athens. You are walking to the market to buy food and perhaps running other errands like paying taxes or meeting a friend. Along comes an ugly, tattered man, shoeless and probably pretty smelly, who stops you to ask a series of questions. "What is the meaning of life?" "What is virtue?" "What is justice?" It's not hard to understand why Socrates earned a mixed reputation in Greece. Yet he increasingly attracted young intellectuals. (He must have had that elusive quality called charisma.) The Socratic method of teaching, named after him, relied on many questions used to draw out pupils' knowledge and guide them toward a philosophical awakening.

Socrates lived for his beliefs and eventually died for them as well. After Sparta defeated Athens in 404 BCE, a cabal of ruthless men took over the city. Not long after that, Socrates, who had grown increasingly unpopular with the new leaders of Athens, was brought to trial on what many believed to be trumped-up charges.

He was accused of corrupting the youth and of not worshipping the city's gods. In actuality, Socrates was part of a conspiracy against the Athenian democracy. Athenian leaders offered to let him go into exile and thus avoid a trial. He refused, went to trial, and was judged guilty and sentenced to death.

Although known through the ages as a philosopher, Socrates recorded not a word of his thinking. Plato, a follower, was present at his trial, but due to his own illness could not witness Socrates' death. Plato preserved the ideas of Socrates, including the account of Socrates' trial, in *Apology*. Other writers who preserved the ideas of Socrates were Xenophon, Aristophanes, and Aristotle.

Socrates believed that after death he would come to a place more worthy and real than life on earth, and so he was at peace with both himself and with the verdict of death by poison. When the time came, he took the cup of poison hemlock and said, "We can and must pray to the gods that our sojourn on earth will continue happy beyond the grave." With those words, he calmly drank the potion.

The symptoms of poisoning came quickly. His heart beat wildly. He began to salivate and sweat profusely. He was dizzy and had a severe headache. Following this period of nervous stimulation, his nervous system began sliding into a depressed phase. His heart rate slowed, paralysis set in, and ultimately he quit breathing and died. And so it was that poison hemlock, a common weed that now grows along many highways and on disturbed land, became forever linked with Socratic philosophy.

Umbels in Literature

William Shakespeare was as literate in the world of herbs as he was in the English language. Parsley (*Petroselinum crispum*), for example, is mentioned in act 4, scene 4, of *The Taming of the Shrew*. Lucentio and his servant Biondello are discussing Lucentio's upcoming marriage to Bianca. There is some question as to whether the marriage will be legal, and Biondello uses the phrase "Cum preuilegio ad Impremendum solem," which some have suggested means, in less than proper Latin, "Stamping one's own image on a woman by getting her with child." Clearly there is some need for haste in getting Bianca together with Lucentio, a priest, and witnesses. For that reason, Biondello says, "I cannot tarry. I knew a wench married in an afternoon as she went to the garden for parsley to stuff a rabbit; and so may you, sir; and so adieu, sir."

In act 4, scene 5, of *Hamlet*, Laertes observes the symptoms of Ophelia's dementia. Ophelia sings ditties and recites the meanings of plants: "There's rosemary, that's for remembrance. Pray you love, remember. And there is pansies, that's for thoughts." Laertes muses, "A document in madness, thoughts and remembrance fitted." Ophelia goes on, "There's fennel for you, and columbines. There's rue for you, and here's some for me." In Shakespeare's time, fennel (*Foeniculum vulgare*) symbolized flattery.

Eryngium is featured in act 5, scene 5, of *The Merry Wives of Windsor*. Mistress Ford says, "Sir John! Art thou there, my deer? My male deer?" The fat, merry, ribald Falstaff, the boastful knight who is also a character in *Henry IV*, replies, "My doe with the black scut! Let the sky rain potatoes; let it thunder to the tune of Green Sleeves, hail kissing-comfits and snow eringoes; let there come a tempest of provocation, I will shelter me here." Although it sounds like Falstaff is pleading for stormy weather, he is really praying for sexual prowess. "Kissing-comfits" are breath fresheners, and "eringoes" are the candied roots of sea holly (*Eryngium* species). In Elizabethan times, eryngiums were considered powerful aphrodisiacs.

A more recent reference to umbels appears in J. R. R. Tolkien's *The Lord of the Rings* (book 1, chapter 11, "A Knife in the Dark"):

> The leaves were long, the grass was green,
> The hemlock-umbels tall and fair,
> And in the glade a light was seen
> Of stars in shadow shimmering.
> Tinuviel was dancing there
> To music of a pipe unseen,

And light of stars was in her hair,
And in her raiment glimmering.

It's not clear whether "hemlock-umbels" refers to water hemlock (*Cicuta maculata*) or poison hemlock (*Conium maculatum*), but the point is that these plants are poisonous. Tolkien mentions hemlock again in the same chapter, and the overall effect is of eeriness and enchantment.

Rudyard Kipling, in the first stanza of "Our Fathers of Old," wrote:

Anything green that grew out of the mould
Was an excellent herb to our fathers of old.

An appropriate reference to the ancient associations of mankind with herbs, don't you think?

Herbs as Symbols

In Victorian times and for some years afterward, there were traditions that called for herbs, flowers, and other plants to represent emotions. This offered friends, lovers, and yes, even enemies a way to express what they felt without coming right out and saying it.

This was especially useful for women at that time, since they were expected to love, honor, and obey, and never—no, never—talk back or act in any unseemly way, especially toward their husbands. Although I rather doubt this was the way things really were, this language of plants allowed one to send a bouquet that was in itself a message.

The Apiaceae was well represented in the catalog of Victorian symbolism. Angelica, for instance, stood for inspiration, while coriander (*Coriandrum sativum*) represented concealed merit. Fennel (*Foeniculum vulgare*) in a bouquet or tussy mussy signaled that the sender thought the receiver worthy of praise. Fool's parsley (probably *Aethusa cynapium*, a Eurasian native now naturalized throughout much of northeastern North America) was synonymous with silliness, while chervil (*Anthriscus cerefolium*) represented sincerity. Garden myrrh (*Myrrhis odorata*), the plant we know as sweet cicely, stood for gladness, and parsley (*Petroselinum crispum*), the best known of all the umbelliferous herbs, symbolized festivity. Hemlock, either water hemlock (*Cicuta maculata*) or poison hemlock (*Conium maculatum*), not surprisingly, meant, "You will be my death." Combining multiple umbels in one bouquet could certainly send a few mixed messages!

Miss Willmott's Ghost

There lived in England a wealthy woman named Ellen Willmott. Born in 1858, she was the daughter of a lawyer and financier who made highly profitable investments in the worldwide railroad boom. Upon her father's death, Miss Willmott inherited the family estate, Warley Place in Essex, as well as plenty of money to support her growing love of plants. When she finished establishing the gardens at Warley Place, she bought a French château and an Italian villa, and designed and planted gardens there, too.

She associated with and became a confidante of royalty and other upper-crust English society, and used contacts such as Edward VII, Queen Mary, and George V to help her in her horticultural pursuits. Rumor had it that she had as many as 104 gardeners working for her at Warley Place alone, and she was known as a taskmaster who would not abide a weed or plant out of place.

In 1897 Miss Willmott's fame and success in horticulture led to her sharing the prestigious Royal Horticultural Society's Victoria Medal of Honour with Gertrude Jekyll. She was honored by many botanists and horticulturists, who named various plants after her, including roses, irises, lilacs, and peonies. The many plants named in her honor were small reward for her generosity in backing botanists and plant-collecting expeditions.

From 1910 to 1914, Miss Willmott contracted to have *The Genus Rosa* published, a body of work with twenty-five parts, all printed on the finest paper and crowned by well more than a hundred water-color illustrations by Alfred Parsons. Although this title and her other work, an excellent collection of prints of the Warley Place gardens, were both losers financially, today they are worth a great deal to collectors, probably well more than $2000 for *The Genus Rosa*.

Miss Willmott grew more eccentric and peculiar as the years went by. While she was influential and an asset to the Royal Horticultural Society, she was, at the same time, imperious and demanding of her nursery contacts. She used people, and if they didn't prove helpful to her, she ignored or insulted them.

As great as the Willmott fortune had been, even it melted away as Miss Willmott continued to spend profligately on her many plant pursuits. By the time she died in 1934, she had been reduced to living in just three shabby rooms of the once elegant three-story Warley Place. Following her death, Warley Place was demolished, and the once cherished gardens fell into ruin.

But to get to the story of Miss Willmott's ghost: In her prime, when she toured others' gardens, Miss Willmott carried with her the seed-like fruitlets of the handsome, silvery bluish green sea holly *Eryngium giganteum* 'Bieberstein'. She loved this plant and secretly scattered the fruitlets as she went along. Thus her trail was often marked by the later appearances of *E. giganteum*, and the species came to be called Miss Willmott's ghost. Later, as she aged, some would say Miss Willmott had become as prickly as the sea holly she loved so much. To this day, at least partly as a result of her energetic sowing, *E. giganteum* is more commonly known and grown in Great Britain than it is in America.

CHAPTER 2

Medicinal and Poisonous Umbels

T HE PLANTS OF THIS FAMILY have a long history as medicinal herbs, stretching back over thousands of years. It is not surprising that many people continue to rely on old, even ancient treatments that call for some of our favorite umbellifers. As you will see, many of the medicinal uses of these plants bear close resemblance to the uses of long ago.

Oddly, although the parsley family includes many healthful herbs, it also includes some of the most toxic plants in the world. The tale of Socrates and his tea of poison hemlock is the best-known historical evidence of this particular plant's lethal attributes. For obvious reasons, this and the other poisonous umbels are important species to recognize, and so these too are discussed in this chapter.

The History of Medicinal Umbels

As humans first learned to use plants medicinally, this knowledge was passed down through the generations by medicine men, shamans, and women. In India and Egypt, records of plants and their medicinal usage date from about 1500 BCE, while records in China date to centuries before that. Dioscorides wrote his *Materia Medica* in the first century CE.

John Gerard's *Herball*, based to some degree on the work of Dioscorides and other men of ancient Greece and Rome, typifies the early herbals, which were among the first printed books following Gutenberg's invention of the printing press. Prior to that, each copy of a book had to be painstakingly hand-copied, word by word.

In this excerpt from *The Herball*, Gerard describes the parsnip (*Pastinaca sativa*) and its effects on the body:

> The parsneps nourish more than doe the Turneps or the Carrots, and the nourishment is somewhat thicker, but not faultie nor bad, notwithstanding they be somwhat windy: thye passe through the bodie neither slowly nor speedily: they neither bind nor losse the belly; they provoke urine, and lust of the bodie; they be good for the stomacke, kidneies, bladder, and lungs.

In another passage he describes some medicinal uses for parsley that stand in contrast to our modern uses for this herb:

> The seeds are more profitable for medicine; they make thinne, open, provoke urine, dissolve the stone, breake and waste away winde, are good for such as have the dropsie, draw downe menses, bring away the birth and after-birth; they be commended against the cough, if they be mixed or boiled with medicines made for that purpose; lastly they resist poisons, and therefore are mixed with treacles.

Herbal Medicine

Herbal medicine was widespread in North America in the sixteenth century, and as European settlers became more numerous, the knowledge of herbal medicine shared by American Indians and Europeans became increasingly integrated. Later, in the nineteenth century, North America's herbal traditions in medicine began to decline because of legislation that required orthodox medical training for herbal practitioners.

While medicine in the United States is more focused upon manufactured drugs, in many parts of the world herbal medicine is still an important practice. In countries such as China, Japan, England, France, and Germany, herbal remedies continue to be prescribed by physicians and are considered the equal of manufactured drugs. The reason for herbal medicine's comparative lack of popularity in the United States has to do with money. In this country, the Food and Drug Administration is responsible for approving medicines, and clinical trials are a requirement. Herbalists may apply to the FDA under current rules, but the procedures are very expensive, and since it is not possible to patent herbs, herbalists are left unable to recover their costs. The total cost of bringing a new pharmaceutical into the marketplace is well over $140 million and may cost as much as $500 million, according to herb guru and expert James Duke.

Research into the medicinal properties of plants has continued to advance since the nineteenth century, and some reviews of medical literature estimate that about 25 percent of the active ingredients in drugs prescribed in 1996 had their origin in flowering plants. A review of plant-derived medicines lists 119 drugs that include ingredients from approximately ninety species.

The following umbels are among those most often used in medicinal treatments of the past. In some cases these plants are still used this way, especially by contemporary herbalists. Anyone planning to use herbal remedies for medical reasons should, of course, first consult a physician. Publications describing herbal remedies often list an alarming number of warnings, interactions, and side effects.

Anethum graveolens (dill; Plates 2 and 3) has served as an important medicinal for at least 5000 years. The early Egyptians used the leaves and fruits to treat digestive problems and soothe colicky infants, and some people still use a dill tea to treat stomach upsets. An old folk tradition says that if you hang a bunch of dill over your door, you will be protected from evil and witches. Poultices of the leaves are said to reduce swelling, including boils, and lessen joint pains. The seed-like fruitlets can also be chewed to sweeten the breath, and some commercial soaps are scented with dill.

Angelica archangelica (garden angelica; Plate 5) is said to have many valuable medicinal properties. All parts of the plant are used. Some authorities approve the use of angelica for treating pleurisy, bronchitis, rheumatoid disease, indigestion, and catarrh. It has also been used to treat exhaustion. Angelica was traditionally thought to have special powers against plagues and poisons. During World War I, people chewed the root, believing it would protect them from the pandemic influenza that killed so many people. In ancient times the Chinese considered this plant the best treatment for gynecological problems. American and European herbalists, as well as those of India and China, still consider it the best treatment for menstrual irregularity and also use it as an aid to digestion and a mild diuretic. It has also been recommended for treating lung ailments, constipation, and kidney ailments. The dried fruitlets are part of the formula for some distilled liquors. The essential oil of the roots also lend a distinctive flavor to some liqueurs, including Benedictine and Chartreuse, which might be considered medicines of a sort.

Apium graveolens (wild celery) is traditionally used to treat arthritis, gout, urinary tract inflammation, and insomnia, usually using the fruitlets in a tincture or infusion but sometimes using the volatile oil. Herbalists have used wild celery to treat flatulence, rheumatism, jaundice, dropsy, mouth ulcers, poisonous spider bites, and even hysteria. Celery also has a long history as an aphrodisiac and diuretic. Early herbalists used all parts of the plant, although they considered the fruits most potent. Boiled leaves were used as poultices to treat wounds. The seed-like fruitlets were favorite sexual stimulants of the ancient Romans.

Carum carvi (caraway) has long been used to aid digestion and treat indigestion and like so many other traditional herbs has also been thought to cure flatulence. Early physicians recommended making an infusion or decoction of the fruits to drink as a remedy for digestive disorders, and caraway was recognized as a treatment to increase lactation in nursing mothers. An odd belief from Europe was that caraway prevented the theft of anything containing it. Farmers would feed caraway to their fowl in the belief that it would keep them from straying. Chewing the seed-like fruitlets will sweeten the breath, and the aromatic essential oils are ingredients in cosmetics, perfumes, and some food flavorings.

Coriandrum sativum (coriander; Plate 12) has been imbued throughout history with magical as well as medicinal properties. The Chinese believed the fruitlets bestowed immortality on those who ate them. It has also been an ingredient of incense used to call up devil spirits. Hippocrates, as well as ancient Egyptians and Indians, used coriander in medicinal preparations. Both fruits and leaves have served as an aphrodisiac, an aid to digestion, and an appetite stimulant. Traditional Indian medicine called for using decoctions of the fruitlets to prevent smallpox, and modern herbalists recommend the same preparation for lowering cholesterol. If taken in excessive amounts, coriander will produce narcotic-like symptoms. Modern studies, including some at the University of California, have shown that the fresh leaves (cilantro) used in Mexican salsas have strong antibacterial and fungicidal properties. When tested in the laboratory, cilantro was discovered to be more effective than the antibiotic drug gentamicin in killing *Salmonella* bacteria.

Ferula assa-foetida (asafoetida) has many medicinal characteristics. The dried gummy sap has traditionally been used to treat asthma, bronchitis, constipation, impotence, flatulence, painful menstruation, and infant colic. Another early tradition says that asafoetida will counteract the effects of opium. Lumps of it were worn by some European ethnic groups as amulets to ward off germs. All parts of the plant are foul-smelling. The sap is harvested by cutting the stem close to the root to allow the juice to ooze out. It is then dried into a reddish yellow gummy substance and processed as a paste, extract, or powder. In what is now Iran, Persian gum gatherers would cut the stem and harvest the dried sap from spring to fall, as many as fourteen times. The gum was shipped to India and, oddly, was not used as a Persian pharmaceutical. Not surprisingly, asafoetida, the product of this odd umbel, is little known outside of Iran and India as an edible or medicinal plant.

Foeniculum vulgare (fennel; Plate 23) also has many medicinal characteristics. The volatile oil extracted from the fruits has long been used to treat coughs, bronchitis, indigestion, and flatulence. In addition, fennel has been used to treat inflammations of the eyelids and conjunctivitis. Ancient Egyptians used it as an aid to dieting, and early Anglo-Saxons chewed it on days of religious fasting. In the seventeenth century, fennel leaves and roots were used to make a tea or broth that promised to curb the appetite. Fennel was an early symbol of success and was one of the plants woven into winners' crowns in athletic competitions. Early Hindus and Chinese used it as an antidote to snake and scorpion bites. Like dill, fennel was believed to repel the evils of Satan, and so early Americans hung it over their doorways to repel witches and other evil spirits. One of the oddest of the old beliefs is that Pliny the Elder thought that snakes looked for fennel to clear their eyesight after shedding their skins. Perhaps that is the origin of using fennel to treat eye ailments. Modern herbalists recommend a tea of the seed-like fruitlets to calm hunger pangs and thus serve as an aid to losing weight. They also suggest fennel for treating fatigue, stomachaches, menstrual cramps, and premenstrual syndrome. Some Africans swear by fennel as a treatment for digestive upsets and diarrhea. In Jamaica it is used to treat respiratory problems.

Heracleum sphondylium subsp. *montanum* (cow parsnip) is an American native that was widely used medicinally by American Indians, who boiled and ate the roots or peeled and ate the tender young stems, whether raw or cooked. Indians taught early American settlers to use pinches of ash from the burned leaves as a serviceable salt substitute. Some tribes also used cow parsnip to drive off the evil spirits that stole good luck from deer hunters. Medicinally the fruits were used for just about everything, from curing headaches to easing toothaches and treating epilepsy. Contemporary herbalists use cow parsnip mainly as a poultice for treating skin irritations and boils. Direct contact with the plant may cause mild dermatitis.

Levisticum officinale (lovage), a strongly aromatic herb, has since ancient times been considered an excellent treatment for gas pains, similar to its cousin *Apium graveolens* (wild celery). Preparations of the root have traditional medicinal uses in promoting urine flow and bringing on menstruation. In addition, skin lotions and washes may include lovage leaves for their soothing qualities. Ancient Greeks chewed the seed-like mericarps to aid digestion, and lovage tea was once used to treat rheumatism. As a culinary herb, the leaves are most commonly used, while the fruits and roots are more often used medicinally.

Petroselinum crispum (parsley; Plate 29) is used medicinally as a liquid extract or infusion. The leaves, stems, fruits, and roots are all used in various treatments. The fruits are used in treating gout and arthritis. The root is taken to ease flatulence, rheumatism, and cystitis. The leaves are soothing when placed on swollen or irritated eyes, and a poultice of parsley will sooth the itch and sting of insect bites. Both jaundice and a persistent cough can be treated with a tea made from the leaves, the roots, or both, according to early herbalists. Modern herbalists use the plant as a stomach tonic, diuretic, and expectorant. Traditionally, it was used to treat digestive disorders as well as inflammation of the kidneys and bladder. It was also used to promote menstruation and ease menstrual pain, as it still is today. The early Greek traditions associated parsley with funerals and death. Superstitions associated with parsley seem downright inane today, such as the belief that disaster would befall anyone who transplanted it, gave it away, or picked it while in love.

Parsley is sometimes used to treat animals as well. For instance, in hoofed animals it can help relieve disorders of the kidneys, rheumatism, constipation, and intestinal obstructions. According to the *Herbal Handbook for Farm and Stable* (Levy 1976), sick sheep and goats should be fed parsley daily in doses of either three handfuls of leaves, three roots, or 2 ounces (56 g) of the seed-like fruitlets. The amounts are doubled or tripled for cattle and horses. Ancient Greeks treated their racehorses with parsley to increase their strength. Both sixteenth-century English herbalist William Turner and early fishing expert Izaak Walton believed that you could cure sick fish by throwing a handful of parsley in the fishpond.

Pimpinella anisum (anise) is used to treat a number of medical conditions, particularly using the fruits and essential oils. Pliny the Elder said that chewing the seed-like mericarps would freshen the breath and improve digestion, and the plant is still used for these purposes. In addition to aiding digestion, the fruits are used to treat and ease bloating, flatulence, nausea, and infant colic, and anise has been used to increase mothers' milk and cure dizziness. As an expectorant and antispasmodic medicine, the fruits have been used to treat coughs, asthma, and bronchitis, and anise remains an important ingredient in cough drops and syrups. Anise oil is used commercially in some mouthwashes and toothpastes. The essential oil, when diluted, is also used to treat lice and mite infections.

Some parsley family plants that were once used medicinally are now extinct, such as the fennel-like *Ferula silphium*, which appears to have become extinct in about the first century CE. This plant apparently grew on the coastal plains of Kyrenaika, where Libya is today, and was used as a food and seasoning but most importantly as a medicine. It was used to treat many ailments, including sore throat, fever, indigestion, seizures, and even leprosy. It was also used in birth control. It had a thick root, a stalk like that of fennel, leaflets like celery, terminal clusters of round, yellow flowers, and heart-shaped fruit called phyllon. An aromatic gum was derived from it, a much valued product in its time.

Poisonous Umbels

This is the other side of the coin—the poisonous species. The parsley family, like the pea family (Fabaceae), includes not only marvelously edible species of human diets but also horribly poisonous plants. Two species, *Conium maculatum* (poison hemlock) and *Cicuta maculata* (water hemlock), are among the world's most dangerous plants for humans. These two umbellifers alone accounted for about 40 percent of North American deaths from plants during the decade beginning in 1985.

The reason for this is easy to see once you think about it. Many species are very similar. For instance, the highly poisonous water hemlock looks very much like the more innocent water parsnip (*Sium suave*), whose roots were long consumed by both American Indians and early European settlers. For this reason it is extremely important to know how to identify both the harmless and hazardous plants of this group. This may be a daunting assignment, since both edible and poisonous umbels are widespread and common throughout much of the world. The safest choice is to refrain from grazing on wild plants. Grow your own favorite umbels or buy them at a farmers market or grocery store.

Experts on poisons have a saying: the poison is in the dose. Many commonly eaten substances (even water!) can cause illness or even death if overused. Poison hemlock and water hemlock have both been used in small amounts in homeopathy. This old system of medical practice is based on the use of minute amounts of a remedy that in large amounts would produce symptoms of the disease being treated. Homeopathy is a controversial subject among many physicians and scientists.

The most dangerous umbels do their damage internally. These are poisonous when eaten, causing a variety of symptoms and even death, depending on the plant and the dose. Symptoms may be neurological or digestive or may cause abnormalities in offspring. The following three umbels cause neurological problems.

Aethusa cynapium (fool's parsley) originated in Eurasia but is now found in southeastern Canada and the United States, mostly the northeastern part, although it has also been reported in Alabama and other places. Since this annual is quite unpalatable and usually occurs where livestock do not graze, it is less of a problem than the poisonous *Cicuta maculata* and *Conium maculatum*. The intensity of the neurotoxins appears to vary considerably depending on environmental conditions, so there are varying opinions as to this plant's degree of toxicity. Fool's parsley has been known to cause early symptoms in animals similar to those brought on by *Conium maculatum*. Symptoms in children include nausea, stomach cramps, diarrhea, and sometimes seizures.

Cicuta maculata (water hemlock; Plate 10) is the lesser poison when compared with *Conium maculatum* (poison hemlock), but even so, this perennial or biennial plant is extremely dangerous in its own right. It is sometimes called poison hemlock, creating yet another confusion over common names. Like the true poison hemlock, water hemlock is a neurotoxic poison, containing a toxin that causes both convulsions and cardiopulmonary failure. The first signs of poisoning include nausea, sweating, and muscle twitching. The poison is most concentrated in the roots, which may, unfortunately, be confused with edible species such as water parsnip (*Sium suave*). Death may occur within eight hours or less after the plant is eaten. Since misidentification is possible, it's best to avoid browsing in the wild. Unlike poison hemlock, water hemlock is found as solitary, scattered plants rather than growing in colonies. This makes it easier to recognize. Plants grow in wet and marshy areas and by rivers and ponds throughout much of North America, even into the cold areas of zones 3 and 4.

Conium maculatum (poison hemlock; Plate 11) is a deadly poisonous biennial plant that I was not personally familiar with when I first started writing this book, although I did know the story of Socrates' death. I'd heard that poison hemlock grew along highways in Indiana. Since I really didn't want to drive a couple of hundred miles to study and photograph it, I was serendipitously delighted one spring to find an 8-foot (2.4 m) colony of poison hemlock while on my way to the local post office. There it was, vigorously growing on the railroad right-of-way, between the tracks and road. It was in full flower, with deeply cut, ferny, pinnate foliage growing robustly from the ridged and purple-spotted stems. According to folklore, the purple streaky spots on the stems represent the mark put on Cain's forehead after he killed his brother.

Since poison hemlock is hardy to zone 5, you won't find it in colder climes, nor will you find it in desert regions: it needs more moisture to grow enthusiastically. You'll find it growing in sun to partial shade in rich, damp soil on roadsides, near water, in open woods, and in similar places. Like thistles, poison hemlock grows as a basal rosette with fern-like leaves during its first year, only reaching its large full maturity during the second year. The plant dies once it is finished fruiting. White flowers grow in large, open, compound umbels that usually appear from May to July.

All parts of poison hemlock are poisonous, containing a number of potent alkaloids, but the poison is especially concentrated in the foliage, roots, and unripe fruit. Children have been poisoned when they make peashooters of the hollow stems, and healthy livestock or wildlife can die from eating a lot of the fresh green plant. Fortunately, drying destroys the harmful alkaloids, and therefore hay containing poison hemlock should not harm animals. Cooking is also said to destroy the poisons. For this reason, ancient Greeks and Arabs were able to use the roasted root as a treatment for joint pain, tumors, and skin diseases.

Other species cause various degrees of irritation and damage by means of photosensitization—that is, external contact with the plants makes the skin supersensitive to sunlight. The genera best known for causing this kind of poisoning are *Ammi* and *Heracleum*. While the effects are seldom fatal in humans or other animals, they can certainly cause an inconvenience when those affected are unable to carry out their daily activities. In lesser cases the poisoning results in what looks like sunburn, while in more severe cases there may be rashes, blisters, and lesions accompanied by severe itching.

The signs of photosensitization usually occur in humans about two days after exposure to the plant. The first sign may be a simple reddening of the skin, followed by more severe symptoms. Changes in skin color may last for several weeks. For both humans and animals, the cure is time.

Luckily, prevention is easy. Search for the possible causes of photosensitization and remove the plants, or see to it that both animals and people stay away from the suspected cause.

In addition to their other effects, poison hemlock and water hemlock may cause photosensitization. To a much lesser extent, *Angelica* species, *Apium* species, and *Sium suave* can also cause dermal reactions, as those who have frequent or extensive contact with these plants can testify.

CHAPTER 3

Edible Umbels

U MBELS HAVE BEEN USED in the culinary arts nearly as long as they have been used medicinally. The family includes a number of favorite culinary herbs, spices, and vegetables, many of which are just as lovely to look at as they are to use in cooking.

The plants discussed in this chapter are all recognized as safe for consumption. However, there are sensitive individuals who may be adversely affected by a specific plant. I must again stress the importance of careful identification when looking at wild plants. Some poisonous wild umbellifers can be easily mistaken for safe and useful plants such as flat-leaved parsley (*Petroselinum crispum* var. *neapolitanum*). As always, proceed with caution.

Herbs and Spices

The culinary herbs of this plant group include a number of favorites commonly used by good cooks as well as a few that are less well known but bear looking into.

Parsley is likely the most common of all the umbelliferous herbs and probably among the first ones we recognize as children. It can be found in just about every produce market, especially the curly type so often used for garnish and then pitched. Like other dark green leafy vegetables, parsley is loaded with vitamins and minerals, and it tastes great as well.

Dill is probably the next most familiar herb of the family, known best for its alliance with cucumbers, that perfect marriage of flavors we know as dill pickles. If you look carefully, you can see the dill's seed-like mericarps and perhaps bits of leaves in the brine of the pickle jar.

Though they are less well known, herbs such as angelica, anise, caraway, chervil, cumin, fennel, and lovage deserve more attention than they usually get. The following list includes these and other culinary umbels.

Anethum graveolens (dill; Plates 2 and 3) is used as an herb. The young bluish green foliage has a delicate taste that adds a nice touch to egg, fish, and poultry dishes. As the plant matures, its seed-like fruits can also be used as a spice. Both foliage and fruits go especially well with cucumbers and potatoes, and the fruits are often used in vinegars and baked goods. Dill is extremely popular in Scandinavia and is much used in India, where it is commonly found in curries, chutneys, soups, and rice dishes. There are a number of cultivars, each varying somewhat in appearance and taste, so it pays to experiment to find your favorite.

Angelica archangelica (garden angelica; Plate 5) is a favorite of many advanced herb gardeners, but its culinary uses are more esoteric than most table herbs. A sweet licorice flavor and aroma permeate the entire plant. All parts of the plant are used—roots, stalks, and foliage. The roots are harvested during fall of the first year, the stalks during the second year before the flowers open, and the leaves anytime during the second year. The fresh leaves can be used in teas, salads, soups, or stews, or as garnish. The dried, ground roots are used in baked goods such as breads, cakes, pies, and cookies. According to some fans of angelica, the young stems are the best part for eating; these can be candied, cooked with rhubarb or tart berries, or added to marmalades and jams. The fruits and roots are used in liqueurs such as Benedictine and Chartreuse.

Anthriscus cerefolium (chervil) is a much noted herb of French cuisine and one of the fines herbes of French cooking. It gains new

praise every time someone begins using it in recipes. Although chervil very much resembles flat-leaved parsley, if you look closely you
will note that the foliage is a lighter green and more delicate. When
used in conjunction with other herbs, chervil seems to intensify the
flavors of the others. Add the leaves to stews, soups, and other dishes
at the end of cooking, since lengthy cooking will make this herb
bitter. By itself, the foliage tastes somewhat like parsley and somewhat like anise.

Carum carvi (caraway) has a long history, having been used for both
medicinal and culinary purposes as far back as 1500 BCE. This
herb is grown not only for its leaves but also for its ridged mericarps, which some would argue make it a spice. The fruits add a
licorice flavor to rye breads, cookies, and candies, while the essential oil is used to flavor foods, cosmetics, and liqueurs. The fruits
can also be used to flavor meat, vegetable, and fish dishes and well
as cheeses and eggs. Although the fruits are of prime importance,
all parts of the plant are edible, adding an almost nutty combination of both dill and anise. The carrot-like leaves and long, thick
taproots can be cooked and eaten as vegetables. Use the foliage in
salads as well.

Coriandrum sativum (coriander; Plate 12) has several uses in cooking. The fruits are treated as a spice and called coriander, while the
strong-flavored leaves are used as herbs and called cilantro or Chinese parsley. The lemon-like flavor of the fruits makes them a valuable spice for baked goods and curries, and they can also be used
in sachets and potpourri. The essential oil from the fruits is used
in the food and cosmetic industries. The pungent, feathery leaves,
said by many to combine a strong sage flavor with citrus overtones,
are keynotes in Latin American, Middle Eastern, and Asian kitch-
ens. "Pungent" is an understatement, as the leaves have a strong,
unpleasant odor to some people (including this writer), especially
in hot, sunny weather. To others, the fragrance is very attractive.

Cuminum cyminum (cumin) is a Mediterranean annual cultivated for its seed-like fruitlets. Prized as a condiment since at least Biblical times, cumin today is an important spice in the culinary arts of Mexico, India, and northern Africa. These plants have delicate, deep green foliage and tiny, white to rose flowers that mature into yellow-brown fruits only 0.25 inch (0.6 cm) long. When the fruits are dried they develop their singular taste, which is reminiscent of caraway.

Ferula assa-foetida (asafoetida) is sometimes called giant fennel, which is exactly what it looks like. Although it is known more for its medicinal characteristics, and although it has a strong sulfurous odor, asafoetida used in small amounts can add positively to the tastes of spicy foods such as curries. Fortunately, the plant's vile odor disappears upon boiling. Because it may be used in small amounts in Iranian, Iraqi, and Indian cookery, asafoetida sometimes appears in Asian markets. Some Asian people use the stems and foliage as a vegetable.

Foeniculum vulgare (fennel; Plate 23) has been in common use as a culinary herb since at least the time of the ancient Greeks. Its delicate anise flavor has a nutty quality to it. The fruits, leaves, and tender stems enhance meat, vegetable, and especially fish and seafood dishes. Add it to cooked dishes at the last minute, since cooking it will destroy the delicate flavor. The beautiful foliage makes a wonderful garnish as well. The essential oil is used commercially to flavor foods and scent soaps and cosmetics. Variety *azoricum* (Florence fennel; Plate 24) is grown for its thickened, celery-like leaf stems, which are used as a vegetable or in salads, either raw or cooked. Variety *dulce* (sweet fennel) is a sweet annual herb.

Levisticum officinale (lovage) might be described as giant celery. It has ribbed stalks like celery, with the stalks branching near the top, and has a celery-like taste and fragrance. The dark green leaves are equally tasty in soups, stews, and salads. The stalks can be used as a vegetable, prepared in the same way as asparagus. The stems can be candied, as with *Angelica archangelica*. In early colonial America the thick roots were candied as well, and served as a special treat. Early Europeans used the roots and fruits as a substitute for pepper to season meats and soups. The essential oil of lovage, like that of so many other umbellifers, is used commercially to flavor foods and drinks and is sometimes an ingredient in cosmetics and perfumes.

Myrrhis odorata (sweet cicely), another of the lesser-known herbs, is well worth checking out since it can be useful in several ways, both ornamentally and in the kitchen. Its rather sweet, tasty flavor and fragrance are a combination of celery and anise. This herb makes a good addition to fruits and desserts such as stewed rhubarb. The soft leaves can be added to salads or used as a handsome garnish, and the roots can be prepared like parsnips. This plant make a good flavoring for fruit drinks, teas, and liqueurs, and a little of the grated root enhances the flavors of quick breads and muffins.

Petroselinum crispum (parsley; Plate 29) is best known as a garnish, a regular part of a plate's presentation but one that is seldom eaten. This is too bad, for parsley is high in nutrients, tastes good, and sweetens the breath. Used medicinally since the time of the ancient Greeks, it is increasingly used in the kitchen, where its flavor is a good addition to just about anything but sweet foods. Although perfectly safe to use in salads and as garnishes, parsley is toxic when consumed in very large quantities, acting as a kidney irritant. The stalks are an important ingredient of a bouquet garni used to flavor stews and casseroles. Parsley's essential oil is also used commercially in foods and finds its way into such things as lotions and shampoos. This species comes in three varieties: variety *crispum* (curly parsley), variety *neapolitanum* (flat-leaved parsley; Plate 30), and variety *tuberosum* (Hamburg parsley). The root of Hamburg parsley is treated as a root vegetable.

Pimpinella anisum (anise) is an aromatic annual herb with a strong licorice flavor. It has been widely used in both medicine and cooking for thousands of years. In the kitchen you can use the seed-like fruitlets either ground up or whole to flavor egg dishes, vegetables, soups, and stews, and the leaves make an excellent garnish or can be added to salads, soups, and stews.

Vegetables

The roots of Hamburg parsley, lovage, Florence fennel, and angelica are considered good vegetables, but they are less well known and far less popular than celery, carrot, and parsnip, the major vegetables of this plant group.

Apium graveolens (wild celery) is known in England as smallage. The medicinal values of *celeri* appear in a ninth-century European poem, and, indeed, until the seventeenth century, celery's value was medicinal. The French began using it as a flavoring in the early 1600s, and by the middle of the seventeenth century, in France and Italy, the stalks and leaves were eaten. At that stage, growers began improving celery by selecting plants with stronger, fatter stalks. By the mid-1700s, Europeans were eating celery stalks regularly, growing the plants in late summer and fall, then keeping them over for winter treats.

Early celery was thought to be better in flavor if the grower blanched the stalks by piling soil around them as they grew. Modern varieties of celery remain green and are considered superior in flavor to the blanched or so-called self-blanching types. Also, we now know that the greener a vegetable is, the more nutrients it has. Celery leaves and stalks are tasty and nutritious as raw vegetables or in salads. Celery adds rich taste and texture to soups and stews. In addition, the seed-like fruitlets are often used to flavor a wide variety of dishes, from salads, stews, and soups to meat, fish, and poultry dishes.

Variety *rapaceum* (celeriac; Plate 8) was developed from the same wild species. It is used not raw but as an excellent addition to soups and stews. Celeriac was first described at the turn of the seventeenth century by Italian and Swiss botanists. Although it has never become very popular in America, it is widely used throughout Europe.

Daucus carota var. *sativa* (carrot; Plate 14) has a long and interesting history. Carrots began as *Daucus carota* var. *carota*, Queen Anne's lace or wild carrot, thousands of years ago. If you dig up the thin, pale yellow root of Queen Anne's lace and crush it, you will notice that it smells just like a carrot. Though the plant is tough and woody when mature, it is passably edible when young and tender. At some point in time, however, the variety *sativa* appeared. This root was much thicker and lacked the woody tissue of the original species, and thus the popular vegetable was born.

The first known mention of carrots occurred some 5000 years ago in middle Asia. Egyptian temple drawings from 2000 BCE show a plant that some experts believe is a carrot. The fruits have been found in ancient Egyptian crypts and in prehistoric Swiss villages. And the ancient Greeks and Romans grew white carrots.

The Greeks used carrots as love potions, believing they would make men more lusty and women more inclined toward men. The Roman emperor Caligula believed this and presented his senate members with a great banquet that included nothing but carrot dishes because he wanted to see them become wildly in rut—obviously a man of weird inclinations.

Although carrots were a food crop for both people and livestock as early as the thirteenth century in Asia, it was not until the Middle Ages that they appeared in Europe. They soon became known not only as a healthful food but also as medicines used to treat many diseases and conditions, from cancerous tumors to sexual disorders to snake bite. In the time of Queen Elizabeth I, carrots were so popular that the ferny tops were often used to decorate ladies' hair and hats.

In worldwide popularity, the carrot is second only to the potato, or so its fans insist. There are even Web sites dedicated to it, such as the extensive World Carrot Museum. Although orange carrots are the favorite, through the years carrots have appeared in many colors, including black, green, red, maroon, white, and yellow.

The orange carrot we know so well appears to have originated in sixteenth-century Holland as a patriotic tribute to William of Orange (1533–1584), also known as William the Silent. He was the Dutch statesman who led his country to independence from Spanish rule in what became known as the Eighty Years War (1568–1648). Plantsmen developed and grew the orange carrot to honor and symbolize their support of William during the war.

Since the orange variety had a superior taste, people soon stopped growing the other carrots. Although there are sporadic attempts to redevelop and market carrots of other colors, thus far they do not seem to win out over our sweet and tasty orange carrots, except as oddities. Carrots of other colors do occasionally make forays into the world of haute cuisine in upscale restaurants, however. I've noticed purple dragon carrots (*Daucus carota* 'Purple Dragon'), for instance, featured at one of my own local eating spots.

Carrots are loaded with beta carotene, the substance that makes them orange and that our bodies transform into vitamin A. In fact, carrots have more beta carotene than any other food except liver. And they are rich in fiber and minerals.

In modern cooking, carrots are used both raw and cooked in many dishes, blending well in soups, stews, and salads. A favorite dessert of many is carrot cake, a sweet, rich treat made with shaved carrots. Although carrot tops are edible, they are seldom used—which seems odd, when you think about it.

Here's a tip from a friend in Canada, regarding cleaning large quantities of carrots. Bring the carrots straight in from the field, still covered with soil. After cutting the tops off, place them in a washing machine. Add a clean towel to prevent bruising and breakage, and toss in some ice cubes as scrubbing agents. Set the water temperature to cold, then set the washing machine on rinse and spin. The result is bright clean carrots and far less work than scrubbing in the sink. This will work for parsnips, beets, and potatoes, too. However, while this is a great idea for those who grow a lot of root crops, I would suggest buying an old second-hand washer for the purpose rather than using your usual machine.

Pastinaca sativa (parsnip) deserves high marks for its delicate, sweet taste and smooth, light texture, yet many people rate this root among their least favorite vegetables. On the other hand, many chefs find that the flavor of parsnip makes it an excellent choice for side dishes or appetizers and a great addition to soups, stews, and salads. It has a long history in the kitchen, going back to ancient Roman times, when it was considered a great delicacy. The long-rooted vegetable was bred and selected into improved, plumper-rooted varieties during the Middle Ages. It has also been commonly used as livestock feed, especially in France. Though parsnip is now most often used in cooking, it is worth noting that this plant was historically thought to be good for the stomach and kidneys and was used to treat colic, since it was said to expel wind from the bowels. It was also a popular internal remedy for consumption, cancer, and asthma.

CHAPTER 4

Ornamental Umbels

I'M DELIGHTED to find that more and more gardeners are using edible and herbal umbels for ornamental purposes, adding such attractive herbs as parsley and dill to mixed ornamental beds, borders, and containers. The ferny foliage of umbelliferous herbs makes a pleasant contrast to plants with bulkier, bolder foliage, and the umbrella-like flower heads have an irresistible symmetry. Try using the small ball carrots as a feathery border, fennels as see-through backdrops, and both flat-leaved and curly parsleys to accent planters of petunias or geraniums. Because of its deep green foliage and tight growth, curly parsley is also an excellent choice as a short border for a colorful flower bed.

When you dare to break out of conformity and see the textures, colors, and forms of plants quite aside from their traditional roles in the garden, you will be able to use plants in new and innovative ways. Invent your own combinations and you are sure to create some winning designs.

Adventurous gardeners will want to try some of the more exotic-sounding umbels, such as *Angelica acutiloba* and the other ornamentals listed in this chapter. Although some of these plants may be tricky to find, successful hunts for seeds and plants will reward you with unusual and beautiful additions to your garden. Your favorite local nursery may not carry bayonet plants (*Aciphylla* species) or masterworts (*Astrantia* species) just yet, but you will find that increasing numbers of plantsmen are seeking out and introducing new plants to our garden palettes. The Internet is another good source when searching for unusual plants.

The following are among the most ornamental umbels for the garden. More detailed descriptions, including cultivation information, are given in chapter 8.

Aciphylla (bayonet plant) species grow primarily in New Zealand, although a few are native to Australia. The leaves are spine-tipped and look more like stiff grass blades than the usual ferny foliage of most parsley family members. The small, star-like summer flowers of white to yellowish green grow in numerous compound umbels up to 1.5 inches (3.75 cm) in diameter. Of the forty or so species, only a few are commonly cultivated. *Aciphylla aurea* (golden Spaniard) grows up to 40 inches (100 cm) tall or more and just as wide. It has dense, sword-like, yellow and green leaves and large, dramatic umbels of brownish gold flowers.

Aegopodium podagraria 'Variegatum' (goutweed) has the reputation of being rampant, often establishing itself all too well. One man's ground cover may well be another man's pesky weed. To its credit, this plant will grow where little else will, in shady spots with poor soil. It makes an attractive edging or ground cover where it can be adequately contained and is a great addition to containerized plantings. As it is grown primarily for its attractive, variegated, green and white foliage, it would be wise to cut off the spring-blooming white flower heads before they go to seed. The alternate leaves have three to nine toothed, oval leaflets. The foliage may be mowed during the growing season to produce fresh new growth.

Angelica acutiloba (dong dang gui) is a native of Asia that is quite new to American gardens, although it has long been used as a medicinal in China and Japan. The white-flowered umbels are very fragrant, adding to the potential of this plant for ornamental beds and borders as well as herb gardens. The ferny foliage is pinnate or bipinnate. This biennial was originally thought to be hardy only to zone 7 but has since been proven to be hardy to zone 4, which greatly increases its appropriateness for cooler climates.

Plate 1. *Angelica* from Elizabeth Blackwell's *A Curious Herbal* (1737). Missouri Botanical Garden Sturtevant Pre-Linnaean Collection

Plate 2. *Anethum graveolens*
(dill) provides interesting
contrasts in both texture and
color alongside *Rudbeckia hirta*
(black-eyed Susan) in an
ornamental bed. Photo by
Cindy Gilberg

Plate 3. A close-up of *Anethum graveolens*
(dill) umbels

Plate 4. *Anethum graveolens* 'Fernleaf' was an All-America Selections winner in 1992

Plate 5. *Angelica archangelica* (garden angelica) is a useful and handsome herb

Plate 6. *Angelica pachycarpa* is an ornamental angelica favored for its glossy green foliage and large white umbels. Photo by Jelitto Staudensamen GmbH

Plate 7. The handsome *Anthriscus sylvestris* 'Ravenswing' has rich, dark red foliage. Photo by Jelitto Staudensamen GmbH

Plate 8.
Apium graveolens
var. *rapaceum*
(celeriac) is widely
used throughout
Europe

Plate 9. *Bupleurum longifolium* subsp.
aureum is valued for its umbels of
green-centered golden flowers
framed by prominent yellow bracts.
Photo by Jelitto Staudensamen GmbH

Plate 10. *Cicuta maculata* (water
hemlock) is an extremely toxic plant

Plate 11. *Conium maculatum* (poison hemlock), another extremely toxic umbel, is the hemlock that killed Socrates

Plate 12. *Coriandrum sativum* (coriander) grows thickly in an herb bed at Missouri Botanical Garden

Plate 13. The white-flowered umbels of *Daucus carota* (Queen Anne's lace) are large and handsome. Photo by Cindy Gilberg

Plate 14. The ferny foliage of *Daucus carota* var. *sativa* (carrot) is pretty enough to use as an edging in a perennial or annual bed

Plate 15. *Erigenia bulbosa* (harbinger of spring) is among the first North American wildflowers to bloom. Photo by Kay Yatskievych

Plate 16. 'Blue Star' is an especially beautiful cultivar of *Eryngium alpinum* (alpine sea holly). Its spiky blue flowers add both color and texture to any garden. Photo by Jelitto Staudensamen GmbH

Plate 17. *Eryngium amethystinum* (amethyst sea holly) has striking, steely blue to amethyst umbels with prominent silver-green bracts atop silver-blue stems. Photo by Jelitto Staudensamen GmbH

Plate 18. *Eryngium giganteum* is the plant of English legend known as Miss Willmott's ghost. Photo by Jelitto Staudensamen GmbH

Plate 20. A close-up of *Eryngium variifolium* shows the exquisite form and color of the umbels

Plate 19. *Eryngium variifolium* (Moroccan sea holly) has showy white veins on dark green leaves, giving the plant a handsome variegated look

Plate 21. *Eryngium yuccifolium* (rattlesnake master) is a favorite of American native plant fanciers

Plate 22. A close-up of the *Eryngium yuccifolium* flower head. Note the prominent bracts and mathematical intricacy of the ball-like umbels.
Photo by Cindy Gilberg

Plate 23. *Foeniculum vulgare* (fennel) in bloom in June. Photo by Cindy Gilberg

Plate 24. *Foeniculum vulgare* var. *azoricum* (Florence fennel) is grown for its thickened, celery-like stems, which are used as a vegetable or in salads

Plate 25. *Foeniculum vulgare* 'Smokey' is a vigorous form of fennel

Plate 26. *Hydrocotyle* species (pennyworts) are favorites of water gardeners

Plate 28. *Oxypolis rigidior* (cowbane) is a slim plant of wetlands and swampy places in the northeastern United States and as far west as Minnesota

Plate 27. *Oenanthe javanica* 'Flamingo' is widely grown as an ornamental ground cover for bogs and alongside water features

Plate 29. *Petroselinum crispum* var. *crispum* (curly parsley) in its second-year blooming period. After blooming and going to seed, it will—as biennials do—die

Plate 30. A close-up of second-year *Petroselinum crispum* var. *neapolitanum* (flat-leaved parsley) in bloom

Plate 31. *Peucedanum officinale* (sulphur weed) bears masses of large, loose, compound umbels of sulfur-yellow flowers. Photo by Jelitto Staudensamen GmbH

Plate 32. *Selinum wallichianum* (milk parsley) grows in tidy clumps that may reach 5 feet (1.5 m) tall. Photo by Jelitto Staudensamen GmbH

Plate 33. *Seseli gummiferum* (moon carrot) is noted for its pink flowers and silvery grayish blue foliage, which turns bronzy pink in the fall. Photo by Jelitto Staudensamen GmbH

Plate 34. *Sium suave* (water parsnip) is widespread throughout much of North America, where it grows in swampy places and shallow water

Plate 35. *Smyrnium perfoliatum* (perfoliate alexanders) has bright greenish yellow flower clusters and stems that seem to grow right through the leaves. Photo by Jelitto Staudensamen GmbH

Plate 36. *Torilis japonica* (Japanese hedge parsley) is a weedy Asian native that has spread throughout much of the United States. Here it is in full flower in June

Plate 37. By autumn *Torilis japonica* has formed its prickly fruits. Photo by Cindy Gilberg

Plate 38. The fruits of *Torilis japonica*, with their hooked stickers, attach themselves to anything that passes by, in this case an Australian shepherd. Photo by Cindy Gilberg

Plate 39. Where *Zizia aurea* (golden alexanders) grows in colonies, it makes a lovely display in spring to early summer. Photo by Cindy Gilberg

Plate 40. If you grow parsley, dill, fennel, or several other umbels, you are likely to find the larvae of the black swallowtail butterfly (*Papilio polyxenes asterius*) feeding on the foliage

Angelica archangelica (garden angelica; Plate 5) can be a spectacular and aromatic addition to ornamental beds and borders. The plant itself grows up to 7 feet (2.1 m) tall and features bright green, toothed, deeply divided foliage that adds great texture to garden settings. In early summer the domed umbels of small, lime-green flowers appear, crowning the plant with highly decorative blooms. This angelica makes an elegant statement at the back of a bed or border but can also stand alone as a handsome focal point or accent plant.

Angelica gigas (purple parsnip) is noted for its large, bulbous, dark purple leaf sheaths, which contrast with the typical pale green angelica leaves. This large biennial has beet-red flower heads up to 4 inches (10 cm) in diameter that appear in the fall and make a strong statement in any garden. Purple parsnip is a thick-stemmed, robust plant, often more than 3 feet (0.9 m) tall and wide. Like all angelicas, the flower heads are marvelous both fresh and dried for arrangements.

Angelica pachycarpa (Plate 6) is a top pick for ornamental beds and borders because of its leathery, pinnate, rich glossy green leaves and large, white, compound umbels. Once this handsome plant matures (which takes about three years, according to some growers) it produces its striking umbels on tall flower stalks. These appear from June to August and are large and flat with green-tinted white flowers that have as much design appeal as the handsome, deeply incised foliage. The leaves are so glossy that they look as if they'd been oiled, which adds to the elegance of the plant. Hardy only to zone 8, *A. pachycarpa* would be a great choice for America's southern gardens. With its tropical look, it would also be a handsome focal point in a container for more northern gardens. Note that it grows up to 3 feet (0.9 m) tall and wide.

Anthriscus sylvestris 'Ravenswing' (cow parsley; Plate 7) is an ornamental standout because of its rich, dark red, fern-like foliage, which adds both texture and color to the garden. This biennial or short-lived perennial grows to 3 feet (0.9 m) tall or more and to about 1 foot (0.3 m) wide. It can star in either containers or garden beds, making a handsome dark accent for a border.

Astrantia (masterwort) species are originally from Europe and western Asia and have been cultivated in Europe since the sixteenth century. *Astrantia major, A. maxima,* and *A. minor,* the three masterworts most commonly grown as ornamentals, are often called Hattie's pincushions because of the look of the flower heads. The simple umbels of small, delicate flowers appear from May through late autumn and look like bursts of stars. Showy bracts surround the flowers, framing them with various colors. Flowers range from greenish white to pink to red. The foliage grows in loose rosettes, with leaves that are palmate and sometimes lobed. These are good plants for sites with sun to dappled shade and richly organic, moist soil. They may serve well along the margins of pools and are good shrubby plants for woodland gardens.

   Astrantia major (greater masterwort), which holds the greatest garden interest, grows to more than 30 inches (75 cm) tall and comes in a number of handsome cultivars, such as 'Hadspen Blood', 'Margery Fish', 'Rubra', and 'Sunningdale Variegated'. For the best color, grow the variegated forms in sunny locations. With *A. major* enjoying growing popularity, there are new cultivars each year. A couple of outstanding more recent introductions are 'Buckland' and 'Roma'.

Bupleurum (thorow-wax) species are good choices for growing against garden walls or fences. The genus includes about a hundred annual, perennial, or shrubby species, including a few that are fairly commonly cultivated. The small flowers of the umbels, often surrounded by ornamental bracts, are most often yellow, though they sometimes have overtones of red or green. The leaves are of several shapes and are simple and entire, unlike most plants of the parsley family.

Bupleurum falcatum (sickle-leaved hare's ear) is hardy to zone 3 and a good prospect for rock gardens. It is a shrubby, woody plant with greenish yellow umbels that are choice in arrangements. Though this plant is used mostly as an ornamental in North America, the root is a major Chinese medicinal used in cold and flu treatments.

Bupleurum fruticosum (shrubby hare's ear) is a large, dense, evergreen shrub with domed umbels of yellow summer flowers. As its origin along the Mediterranean coast might suggest, it is a good choice for a seaside garden. I imagine it would also serve well in sites near roads and drives where salt is applied during icy spells in winter months. This species is hardy only to zone 7 and so would have to be treated as an annual in more northern climes.

Bupleurum longifolium subsp. *aureum* (Plate 9) is a knockout. Its golden flowers have green centers, and prominent bright yellow bracts frame each umbel. Like many others in the family, the cut flowers are excellent components of arrangements both fresh and dried.

Bupleurum rotundifolium (thorow-wax) is an erect, bushy plant with foliage reminiscent of eucalyptus. The flowers, with their yellow-green bracts, are attractive additions to either fresh or dried arrangements. The cultivar 'Green Gold' is noted for its vibrantly colored flowers.

Eryngium (sea holly) species are not used nearly enough in American gardens. These are striking plants of unusual structure. Their leaves are often deeply divided and oval to cordate, and most sea hollies have basal leaves that are spiny. The signature umbels of these plants have large bracts and are crowded into dense, domed flower heads that resemble teasel or thistle. The flowers are often white or blue, with the colors more intense in regions where nights are cool. Fresh or dried, the flowers are long-lasting and add a distinctive quality to arrangements. If you cut the top flowers as soon as they are past their prime, chances are the side branches will flower sooner. The sea hollies, true to their name, are good choices for seaside gardens, as they are tolerant of salt sprays. They also naturalize well in beds and borders. The following are a few of the better-known ornamental species.

Eryngium alpinum (alpine sea holly) has bluish green foliage and stems. The mature flowers are a strong blue, with prominent bracts that are pale blue at first but darken with age. Perennial expert Allan Armitage (1997) says, "For flower power, this is the best species." There are several good cultivars.

Eryngium amethystinum (amethyst sea holly; Plate 17) is noted for its cold hardiness (zone 2) and its steely blue to amethyst umbels, which appear in summer with prominent silver-green bracts atop silver-blue stems. The unusual texture of this spiny plant makes a nice contrast to the smoother perennials found in most ornamental gardens.

Eryngium caucasicum (bluetop sea holly), as its common name suggests, is very blue. True blue is unusual in garden ornamentals, making this a fine plant for contrasting accents.

Eryngium giganteum (Miss Willmott's ghost; Plate 18) is large and striking, with steely blue flowers crowned by large, silver-gray bracts. With its pale green foliage, this plant does look rather ghostly. 'Silver Ghost' is a good shorter form.

Eryngium leavenworthii (Leavenworth eryngo) is quite new to ornamental gardens. It is a stunning plant for annual or mixed beds and borders, bearing utterly fantastic purple flower heads that are great for fresh or dried arrangements. The tiny flowers have white to blue-violet petals, and the bracts are spiny and purple. There are hints of purple throughout the plant.

Eryngium variifolium (Moroccan sea holly; Plates 19 and 20) is an unusual evergreen species with handsome variegation, its dark green leaves marked by showy white veins. Blue-gray flower heads are framed with grayish silver-green bracts. This is a good prospect for rock gardens.

Eryngium yuccifolium (rattlesnake master; Plates 21 and 22) is not as spectacular in either color or form as some of the other sea hollies, yet it enjoys great popularity among fans of American native plants. This smooth-surfaced perennial features soft white to pale blue, cylindrical umbels with larger pointed bracts.

Heracleum (cow parsnip) comprises some sixty tall, vigorous biennial and perennial species, including *H. mantegazzianum*, which, though originally treated in American gardens as an ornamental, is now listed as a noxious weed. The large, ornamental leaves of these plants are crowned by large, compound umbels of white flowers in summer. The leaves may be pinnate or palmately lobed. Be careful when handling plants of this group, which produce a clear sap that may cause photodermatitis. Also avoid eating them, as that will cause extreme abdominal pain.

Heracleum sphondylium subsp. *montanum* (cow parsnip) is a biennial or perennial native to northern North America, Europe, and Asia. It easily grows to 8 feet (2.4 m) tall or more. Summer flowers in compound umbels may be white to pale yellow or pale green, often with hints of pink. Contact with this plant may result in dermatitis, but symptoms will be less severe than those caused by *H. mantegazzianum*. Many lovers of native plants like to grow this parsley family member.

Hydrocotyle (pennywort; Plate 26) species are favorites of water gardeners, with the exception of the weedy *H. sibthorpioides* (lawn pennywort). They usually grow to about 4–6 inches (10–15 cm) tall, forming low, semi-evergreen mats of foliage that can provide desired shade to the water surface. The round leaves are quite unlike those of most umbellifers, having their petioles grow from under the centers. The small umbels that appear in spring to summer bear tiny, white flowers. These are great plants for aquariums, garden ponds, and pools. They are easy to grow, and because they do not need to be rooted, they can serve as floating plants that offer hiding places for young fish.

Myrrhis odorata (sweet cicely) is another herb that deserves to be used ornamentally much more than it is. It is a handsome choice for shady ornamental gardens, especially in cooler regions. The fernlike leaves are oblong, lanceolate, and deeply toothed. In early summer, white flowers appear, growing in large, inverted, compound umbels. Elegant in texture and design, these hairy perennial plants are handsome in woodland settings, where they make attractive backgrounds for primulas, bleeding hearts, and the like. The plants grow 2–4 feet (0.6–1.2 m) tall, and the foliage remains sturdy and beautiful well into fall.

Oenanthe javanica (water dropwort) has celery-like, usually pinnate leaves and inverted, compound umbels of small, white flowers that appear in summer. It is native from India to Japan, Malaysia, and northern Australia, growing in moist to wet areas. This plant is most widely grown as an ornamental ground cover for bogs, water gardens, and alongside water features. It grows to 6–8 inches (15–20 cm) tall and thrives in shallow water. 'Flamingo' (Plate 27) is an attractive cultivar with white, pink, and green foliage. Although some people consider water dropwort edible, I wouldn't try it: *Oenanthe* species have been known to cause discomfort when eaten, and some may be deadly. Although *O. javanica* appears to be the exception in its native lands, where it is used as a salad vegetable, plenty of other salad crops are more reliable and tasty, so why mess with a genus that has species known to be poisonous?

Peucedanum officinale (sulphur weed; Plate 31) is noted for its leathery, finely divided leaves and loosely constructed umbels of sulfur-yellow flowers. It may grow to a height of 4 feet (1.2 m), and its feathery foliage has an excellent ornamental quality. A good choice for seaside gardens or more northern gardens that may be exposed to road salt, up to zone 5.

Selinum wallichianum (milk parsley; Plate 32), from India, Pakistan, and China, is noted for its very finely feathered foliage, red stems, and handsome, white-flowered summer umbels. It grows up to 5 feet (1.5 m) tall in tidy, upright clumps. Although only hardy to zone 8, this plant is worth growing as an annual in colder climates. In the garden it will mix well with such plants as salvias, chrysanthemums, and coneflowers. Its flowers and fruits are choice for flower arrangements, whether fresh or dried.

Seseli (moon carrot) species are comparatively new to American perennial gardens. The leaves of these perennials and biennials are feather-like, with slender petioles that grasp the stems. *Seseli gummiferum* (Plate 33) is particularly attractive for its pink flowers and bronze-pink fall foliage. The basal rosette of foliage is a silvery grayish blue. The deeply dissected foliage that grows on the thick stems is valued for its decorative qualities. The compound umbels have silvery white flowers in their outer ring. The flowers open pink in midsummer to fall but fade to white as they age. All in all, *S. gummiferum* and other moon carrots are lovely plants worth searching for.

Smyrnium perfoliatum (perfoliate alexanders; Plate 35) features large, bright greenish yellow umbels. This is a wonderful biennial plant for flower arrangers, offering ornamental flowers and fruits. The leaves are circular on stems that seem to grow right through the leaves. The spring or summer flowers grow in compound umbels. A word of warning: Although introduced as an ornamental, this plant has been known to persist in a weedy manner.

Designing with Umbels

Ornamental umbels can be grown in containers or in garden beds and borders. Many of them add unusual elements of design—color, mass, and form—to the overall composition of a garden. Define the plants' roles and potential sites in your garden and use their individual attributes, applying the elements of design.

Angelica species are large plants, often as wide or wider than they are tall. Their mass, therefore, is on a par with medium to large shrubs. Their outline, because of the deeply serrate, feathery foliage, is itself irregular and finely cut. In color the angelicas range from bright green to dark purple to variegated. The ferny texture of the foliage can be a handsome contrast to the linear quality of ornamental grasses or the simple, entire leaves of salvias and hibiscuses. The overall form of angelicas is imposing, making them good plants to use not only as tall back-of-the-border subjects but also as accents and focal points. Finally, the large umbels of the angelicas add vigorous, bold notes to the garden when they are in bloom. These are among the borderline plants that may be biennial or short-lived perennials. You can encourage their persistence in the garden by seeing that the ripe fruits, each with its pair of seeds, get shaken onto the soil where you want them to grow.

Astrantia (masterwort) is another good group of garden specimens. These perennials grow to 1–3 feet (0.3–0.6 m) tall, depending on the species, and have foliage of a rich green that is palmate to lobed. While the foliage is handsome in itself, it is the profusion of star-like flowers that most recommends these plants. White, green-tinged white, pink, and red flowers in a wide range of values and intensities make these plants ornamental assets for just about any garden. The umbels rise above healthy, compact clumps in a very showy manner. Because of their mass and form, masterworts stand out in a garden setting, blending well with plants of contrasting foliage patterns and colors.

Eryngium (sea holly) species are hard to resist with their rigid, spiny leaves and unusual umbels surrounded by spiny bracts. They range in size from only 15 inches (37.5 cm) tall to well over 4 feet (1.2 m), making them useful at the back of the border as well as in the middle and front, depending upon the particular species or cultivar. The umbels, with small flowers held in rounded or oblong heads, come in a spectacular array of colors, from greens and blues to purples with heavy overtones of silvery gray. Both the irregular outline and colors of these plants make them top choices as accents or focal points. Use them singly in containers or in groups of three or five in a border or bed. These are plants you can use in dry sites, coastal gardens, and even along walkways that are treated with ice removers.

Analyzing prospective plants in this way will result in better design and thus a more successful and beautiful garden. Keep in mind, however, that even when you do everything right, sometimes a particular planting will end up disappointing in its overall effect. That's the time to remember that gardens are ongoing projects, which means they are always changing and always moving from one effect to another. If a plant ends up not creating the glory that was intended, simply move it to another location where it may prove to be a star in its own right. A good time to move the plant "furniture" in your garden rooms is in the fall when any summer drought should be over and night temperatures are cooler.

Finally, when growing these wonderful plants, remember that most of them are excellent prospects for use in either fresh or dried arrangements. Add your favorites to a cutting garden or harvest them directly from your mixed beds and borders. Both foliage and umbels have their own design values. The umbels may be used in arrangements at most stages of development, from buds through ripe fruit heads. If they are already fully ripe, you can probably use them as they are. If they are still green, cut them and hang them upside down singly or in small bunches in a dark place that is not humid. They should be dry and ready for decorative use within a couple of weeks.

CHAPTER 5

Umbels in the Wild

Some of the umbels found growing in a particular wild area originated there and are considered native. Other plants are considered introduced or adventive, even if they emigrated many hundreds of years ago.

Many adventive plants came to the New World as fruitlets in hay and grain destined for animal feed. Old World plants were also introduced after traveling in ships' ballast. In some cases people deliberately introduced plants from other parts of the world, mostly for their ornamental qualities. Once introduced, these plants traveled in all directions, hitching rides on pioneers' wagon trains and later on railroad trains, trucks, and automobiles. Even today, plants continue to move around the continent via every mode of transportation.

This chapter covers the various types of parsley family plants that grow in the wild, including natives, endangered or threatened species, and weeds. Water hemlock (*Cicuta maculata*) and poison hemlock (*Conium maculatum*), both of which are described in chapter 2 as extremely toxic species, are adventive weeds in North America and so are also included here. These plants deserve special attention since they are so very dangerous.

North American Natives

Native North American umbels are a varied group. On the one hand is the delicate, ferny wild chervil, and on the other is the buxom, sturdy rattlesnake master. These plants grow in a range of environments, from dry, rocky soil to the rich, alluvial soils of river bottoms. You can even find some of them growing in water.

The roles these umbels play in their natural environments are varied but generally fall into two categories: food and shelter. The seed-like fruitlets of umbellifers, including native, cultivated, and introduced species, are part of the diet of a number of birds and small mammals. The large quantities of small flowers held in the umbels also hold nectar and pollen that are important for the diets of many insects. For instance, in July and August, the round, whitish flowers of rattlesnake master are an excellent nectar source for butterflies, bumblebees, and other insects. In addition to having nutritious nectar and pollen, the flowers are easily accessible and offer convenient landing pads for a number of bees, wasps, and flies.

Below are a few of the more choice North American natives. There are many others, of course; these few are simply meant to get you started. I have listed several good field guides in the bibliography ("Further Reading") for anyone interested in learning more about these and other native plants.

Chaerophyllum procumbens (wild chervil) is an annual common in the rich, moist soils of wooded river bottoms, valleys, and roadsides. It grows in colonies that may in some places appear to cover the forest floor. If not found in large colonies, it will be easy to overlook. The small umbels of tiny, white flowers appear in springtime. The fern-like leaves are deeply cut and a tender pale green, slightly paler underneath. Some butterfly larvae eat the foliage. You can find this plant throughout the northeastern quadrant of the United States.

Cryptotaenia canadensis (honewort) is a perennial most often found in rich soils of low, woodsy locations, often by streams or creeks. It has smooth, serrate leaves and tiny, white flowers in small, compound umbels.

Erigenia bulbosa (harbinger of spring; Plate 15) is often overlooked because of its small size, but it truly is a harbinger of spring in that it is among the first American wildflowers to bloom, often appearing as early as February. It is native to the northeastern United States from western New York and Pennsylvania to Minnesota and south from there, and also grows in southern Ontario. It is quite common along wooded stream bottoms and in wooded valleys. A tuberous perennial, it has ferny foliage with deeply cut leaves that have three leaflets each. Small umbels bear white flowers with red-brown stamens.

Eryngium yuccifolium (rattlesnake master; Plates 21 and 22) is a perennial native that grows over a large range, from Connecticut to Florida and west as far as Minnesota and Texas. It was once thought to heal snakebites (thus the common name), but I wouldn't count on that actually being the case. You'll find rattlesnake master in prairies, open woods, and glades growing up to 4 feet (1.2 m) tall. A favorite wildflower, it is increasingly finding its way into ornamental gardens.

Osmorhiza longistylis (aniseroot) is a carrot-like, tuberous root native throughout much of the United States, from the Midwest to the East Coast. The stems are smooth to sparsely hairy, and the leaves are biternate and range from finely hairy to almost shaggy. Aniseroot grows in woods and has blackish, club-shaped fruits that will cling to fur or clothing. Small umbels of white flowers appear in spring and early summer.

Oxypolis rigidior (cowbane; Plate 28) is a slim plant found in the northeastern United States from New York to Minnesota. It is known as cowbane because its roots and leaves have been known to poison cattle. Contact with the plant also causes dermatitis in some people. Cowbane grows in moist soils along streams and in swampy areas and wet prairies. The leaves have five to nine slim, lanceolate leaflets that are smooth-surfaced, glaucous, and very lightly toothed. The whitish bloom easily rubs off. White flowers appear from summer to early fall.

Perideridia americana (wild dill) is a perennial native of the American prairie and is considered endangered by some groups. The leaves are pinnate to tripinnate and entirely hairless. The leaflets are thin, almost thread-like. Small, white flowers are in compound umbels.

Sanicula odorata (black snakeroot) grows in woodsy locations throughout much of the northeastern United States. It has compound leaves with toothed, lanceolate leaflets. Summer flowers of a green-yellow grow in burr-like forms in loose umbels up to about 2 inches (5 cm) in diameter.

Sium suave (water parsnip; Plate 34) is native to the northern United States but also grows wild in Canada and eastern Asia. This perennial can be found in swampy places and in the shallow water of streams and ponds. It is invasive and so is also listed as a weed. Though it is technically edible, avoid consuming this plant, which is thought to be poisonous to livestock.

Zizia aurea (golden alexanders; Plate 39) is native from eastern Canada to the southern United States. This widely distributed, adaptable perennial grows up to 24 inches (60 cm) tall. The leaves are bi- or triternate, with leaflets that are finely toothed, and umbels of golden flowers appear in spring to early summer. You can find golden alexanders in open woods, prairies, glades, and fields. The flower petals typically fold in upon themselves. These plants usually grow in colonies and thus are striking when in bloom.

Endangered and Threatened Natives

The designation of plants as endangered or threatened is not the same everywhere. It depends on the mandates of the organization doing the designating, and different organizations have different missions. Further, plants might be endangered in one area but not another. More is being done every year to protect endangered plants and animals, but the work also varies greatly from country to country and from organization to organization.

The U.S. Endangered Species Act of 1973 strengthened previous provisions. Key to my particular focus are the provisions of this act that defined categories of "endangered" and "threatened" and also dictated that plants were eligible for protection. The act mandated that all federal agencies undertake programs for the conservation of endangered and threatened species. The U.S. Fish and Wildlife Service has the primary responsibility for maintaining the data on those species in jeopardy.

The Nature Conservancy created the first natural heritage program, dedicated to defining and preserving endangered species, in 1974. Two decades later, in the mid-1990s, the conservancy spun off the national network of state natural heritage programs as an independent organization known as NatureServe.

NatureServe, a non-profit conservation organization, oversees an international network of natural heritage programs and maintains heritage program protocols among the state national heritage programs, which are usually part of state agencies, such as the Missouri Department of Conservation. NatureServe national heritage programs are a leading source of objective scientific information about both species and ecosystems. This information is used by many sectors of many countries to make wise decisions about the management of natural resources.

The Center for Plant Conservation (CPC), founded in 1984, is a good example of the work being done in conservation. With its headquarters at the Missouri Botanical Garden, the CPC comprises a network of more than thirty botanical institutions dedicated to informed management and the conservation and restoration of native plants. These institutions maintain the National Collection of Endangered Plants, which is represented by plant materials and seeds of more than 600 native United States plants in danger of extinction. The collection continues to expand, and the CPC estimates that an additional 1000 plants will need to be added as soon as possible. In the United States about a dozen native species from the Apiaceae are listed as endangered by the CPC.

The various member institutions work with endangered plants both in the wild and at their own sites, conducting plant research and learning how to grow the plants. They then provide plants for restoration in the wild. The CPC believes that off-site storage and cultivation of genetically appropriate plants is a critical step in supporting restoration of endangered native plants.

Invasive species, habitat loss, overcollection, and disease threaten the existence of many of America's native plants. One in ten native species deserves some concern for conservation. Five percent are on or qualify to be on the federal list of endangered species. Many of these are found in twenty or fewer sites, and some have experienced steep declines in populations.

The following are a few of the umbels listed as endangered by both the CPC and the U.S. Fish and Wildlife Service. Unfortunately, more plants are added to the list every year. At the same time, botanists are learning more about the need for preserving these plants and are dedicating increasing amounts of time to the subject.

Aletes humilis (Colorado aletes) is an endangered plant of cliffs and granite outcroppings in north-central Colorado near the Wyoming border. Researchers have looked in likely places for this rarity for over a century, yet have found it in only seven locations on Colorado's Front Range. It was first discovered in 1898 in Larimer County (thus another common name, Larimer aletes). It is likely that fewer than a dozen colonies of these perennial plants exist today. That it has survived at all is undoubtedly due to its thick, leathery leaves and its habit of growing into low mats of vegetation. These traits conserve moisture, which is important for anything growing in this arid region. Part of this plant's range is in The Nature Conservancy's Phantom Canyon Preserve, but the primary custodian is Denver Botanic Gardens. These two organizations have cooperated in collecting seeds and growing the plants both at Phantom Canyon and at the botanic gardens. Their studies suggest that the Colorado aletes may live for several decades.

Eryngium aristulatum var. *parishii* (San Diego button celery) is an annual with a low, spreading habit of growth and greenish umbels of small flowers that appear in late spring. It is native to California salt marshes and vernal pool systems, which are wet in the winter and dried out by summer. It will germinate during the season of flooding and bloom as the pools begin to dry out, a pattern that is typical of vernal pool plants. The problem for San Diego button celery is that more than 23 percent of the vernal pool systems in California were destroyed by the late 1980s. It currently grows only on the Santa Rosa Plateau in Riverside County, and this single location has only four populations and probably fewer than 1000 individual plants. In the early 1990s, Rancho Santa Ana Botanic Garden, primary custodian for this plant, and the University of California Botanical Garden in Berkeley created a number of small vernal pools for both display and as part of their endangered species program. Since the recreated pools require careful maintenance, they are not self-sustaining and thus will not be able to replace the natural vernal pools. The habitat on the Santa Rosa Plateau Ecological Reserve that supports these threatened plants has received the critical habitat designation that will help support the San Diego button celery.

Eryngium constancei (Constance's coyote thistle) is a slender, low-growing annual found only in northern California. The best-known population grows in two vernal pools in Loch Lomond Ecological Reserve in Lake County (thus two additional common names, Loch Lomond button celery and Loch Lomond coyote thistle). Another population was discovered in 1996 in a couple of shallow, spring-fed ponds in Sonoma County. Loose umbels of small, white to pale purple florets appear in spring. Populations of this eryngium are threatened by erosion due to logging and are also at risk due to planned reservoir construction, off-road vehicles, and development.

The University of California Botanical Garden, the primary custodian of this plant, recognizes the need for seed collection, further study, and protection from runoff. Since logging has increased soil erosion at the Lake County site, a berm has been constructed to eliminate the runoff.

Eryngium cuneifolium (snakeroot) is an erect plant with narrow, wedge-shaped leaves that are long and stalked. It grows only on the southern Lake Wales Ridge in Highlands County, Florida, a scrubby habitat in Florida's xeric upland region. These plants prefer sunny sites of disturbed areas or open sand. Threats include land development for both housing and citrus production, and fire suppression that allows the upper canopy of trees to close over. Historic Bok Sanctuary, the primary custodian for this endangered species, has plants on display in its gardens. Research management includes studies of the effects of land disturbance on the survival of these plants, establishment of additional sites for small populations on protected land, and controlled burning or other mechanical means to maintain the needed open space for habitat.

Lilaeopsis schaffneriana var. *recurva* (cienega false rush) is a semi-aquatic, herbaceous perennial that grows in the cienegas (marshy wetlands) of Arizona. This grass-like plant forms rhizomes that creep along streambeds and eventually form dense mats. It seldom flowers except when the habitat drastically dries out. When it does, the flowering umbels, which may appear from March to October, grow from rhizome nodes and bear three to ten small, greenish florets, which develop into red fruits by late fall. This plant thrives at altitudes of 4000–6000 feet (1200–1800 m) where winters are mild, stream gradients are gentle, and there is year-round water. During cool months, cienega false rush is considerably reduced but resumes growth in March. It appears to spread vegetatively when small plant fragments drift downstream and take root. If plant competition becomes severe and roots are crowded, this lilaeopsis will decline. Threats includes the general loss throughout Arizona of cienega and stream habitats as well as flash flooding and watershed degradation due to grazing and development. The primary custodian is the Desert Botanical Garden in Phoenix, which has growing plants on display. Wild colonies are regularly monitored, but there is a critical need for establishing a seed bank of this plant since it has seldom flowered under cultivation.

Lomatium bradshawii (Bradshaw's desert parsley) was once common in the extensive prairies of the Willamette Valley in Oregon, where it painted carpets of bright sulfur-yellow each spring, growing in moist meadows and prairie patches at low elevations. Later this perennial native was thought to be extinct, but it was rediscovered in 1979 by a University of Oregon graduate student. Most populations are within a 10-mile (16 k) radius of Eugene. Further populations exist in the central and southern Willamette Valley in Benton, Lane, Linn, and Marion counties, Oregon, and in the Puget Trough in Clark County, southwestern Washington. Threats to this plant include land development for housing and agriculture, pesticides that kill pollinators, non-native plant invasion, cattle grazing, and invasion of shrubs due to fire suppression. The Berry Botanic Garden of Portland, Oregon, is primary custodian for this endangered species and has monitored populations and studied the various effects of human intrusion. They have the plant on display as well. The researchers here realize that they must continue monitoring to learn the long-term impact of various grazing intensities. There is also a need for regular burning or other mechanical control of trees and brush. Finally, there is always a need to ascertain reliable methods of propagation and reintroduction.

Lomatium cookii (Agate Desert lomatium) features inconspicuous, green, feathery leaves, and, indeed, this species was only discovered in the 1980s. Once it is in flower, the creamy yellow blooms make it easy to see. Populations exist in the Klamath Mountains of Oregon, specifically in the Agate Desert of Jackson County and the Illinois Valley of Josephine County. This plant lives in vernal pools and so has adapted to grow, flower, and set seed during the short time that water is available in the spring. Threats include habitat loss due to development, ATV use, livestock grazing, woody plant encroachment due to fire suppression programs, herbicide spraying, and logging. As with *L. bradshawii*, the Berry Botanic Garden is the primary custodian. In addition to monitoring the wild populations, researchers are collecting seeds, learning to grow the plants, and learning more about managing both cultivated and wild plantings. They are working to determine both propagation and reintroduction methods.

Lomatium erythrocarpum (red-fruited desert parsley) is a tiny plant that grows high in the Blue Mountains of eastern Oregon. The Berry Botanic Garden is its primary custodian. Being so small, at a maximum 2.8 inches (7 cm) tall, and having foliage of a dull olive-green, this lomatium is rarely noticed except when in flower or fruit. The spring flowers are mostly white or purplish white with flecks of red-purple. The red fruits are up to 0.3 inch (0.75 cm) long. All populations of this plant are in roadless areas of U.S. Forest Service land, and currently there is no active management program. Berry, however, realizes the need for collecting seeds and developing reintroduction programs, as well as for studying the general biology of the plants and learning more about population locations and trends.

Oxypolis canbyi (Canby's cowbane) is a rare perennial herb with quill-like leaves and slender stems. Native to the coastal plains regions of Delaware, Maryland, North Carolina, South Carolina, and Georgia, it grows in cypress savannas, pond shallows, sloughs, and wet pine savannas. Populations are mostly reproduced by means of the strong, fleshy rhizomes, although the plants do occasionally have compound clusters of small, white flowers in August and September. Threats include loss of wetland habitat due to drainage and development, collection, and predation by black swallowtail butterfly caterpillars, *Papilio polyxenes asterius* (Plate 40). North Carolina Botanical Garden, the primary custodian for this endangered species, is attempting to protect the habitat where known populations occur and is monitoring plots in North Carolina. There remains much to be done, from the collection of seeds from various populations to learning the best methods of reintroduction and understanding the biology of the plants' pollination.

Perideridia erythrorhiza (red-root yampah) is native to Oregon's Cascade Range and was once eaten by the American Indians of the region. This perennial grows in moist prairies and pastureland at lower elevations on the west side of the mountains. On the east side, it most often grows in high meadows and at the edges of coniferous forests. The summer umbels of tiny, white flowers are showy and attract many pollinators, including flies and native bees. Threats to red-root yampah include housing developments, grazing, and herbicide application. The western populations are more endangered than the eastern ones because they are fragmented, small, and often on private land, thus not subject to federal and state regulations. The Berry Botanic Garden, primary custodian for this plant, collects seeds and is introducing plants onto Bureau of Land Management land. They will continue to study the plant, collect the seeds, and learn more about effective germination and propagation procedures.

Ptilimnium nodosum (harperella) is a rare and delicate endangered perennial that grows 6–36 inches (15–90 cm) tall along the rocky shoals of clear, swift streams. Its hydrological requirements are very narrow: it needs water that is of good quality and of exactly the right depth. The ten known populations are in scattered locations in Alabama, Arkansas, Georgia, Maryland, North Carolina, South Carolina, and West Virginia. The umbels of tiny, white flowers are similar to those of *Daucus carota* (Queen Anne's lace), but the leaves are not fern-like but rather like short, hollow, quill-like structures. Not surprisingly, the threats to this species are pollution and changes in stream hydrology, such as the draining of the habitat upstream for conversion to agriculture or drowning the habitat through impoundment. North Carolina Botanical Garden, the primary custodian for harperella, is attempting to propagate this endangered plant, but this has been difficult, since, as with many wetland plants, the seeds do not store well. With germination so difficult, much more must be learned if this plant is to be successfully grown and reintroduced.

Weedy Umbels

Every family has its black sheep, or at least its less appealing members, and so it is with the umbellifers. Of course, with plants as with people, beauty is in the eye of the beholder, and many of the weedy umbels can be good additions to the garden. Be sure to use extreme care, however, when planting any that have a tendency to spread rampantly.

It is interesting to note that the majority of our weedy plants, including the weedy umbels, have been introduced from Eurasia. Like our ubiquitous starlings and English sparrows, they have come from a place where they were likely in balance with the rest of the biota, to a continent where they may outcompete many of the natives.

Weeds usually grow on what is called disturbed land, including uncultivated places that used to be under cultivation, places where construction has recently taken place, neglected pastures, and similar sites. Control of weeds is usually easy without resorting to pesticides. Mowing seedlings will break the biennials' cycle since the first-year plants then do not survive to produce seed in their second year. To control annual and perennial weeds, it is also necessary to mow before the plants set seeds. Pulling and hoeing are other tried and true methods for controlling weeds in gardens.

If all else fails, an application of a non-selective herbicide containing glyphosate, such as Roundup, will slay any pesky weeds. But remember that this kind of herbicide will kill any plant when applied to green foliage; it is translocated from the green leaves into the entire root system. Be careful to apply it only to the plants you wish to kill, and never apply any pesticide on a windy day.

The following are examples of weedy umbels. My inclusion of Queen Anne's lace (*Daucus carota*) might come as a surprise to some readers. Like many of the plants that arrived with early settlers, Queen Anne's lace has been growing in North America so long that most people would expect to see it listed as a native. It originated in Europe, however, probably arriving in the New World during the seventeenth century as fruitlets in cattle feed, in straw and hay, and as unwanted extras in collections of seeds to be planted. A case might also be made for listing this plant as an ornamental, since so many gardeners are adding it to their beds and borders. However, I have placed Queen Anne's lace among the weeds, because in the United States it has adapted so well to such a wide variety of habitats that it has spread, in many cases rampantly, throughout much of the country.

Aegopodium podagraria (goutweed), originally from Europe and western Asia, is a creeping plant with enthusiastic rhizomes. It is often a choice of perennial gardeners, who use the variegated form ('Variegatum') as both an edging and a ground cover. Unfortunately, this plant has a tendency to escape gardens and is therefore considered by many to be a weed. In the past I have grown the variegated form for its green and white patterns. It didn't take long to become disenchanted, however, as the plant's creeping rootstocks crept everywhere. Although it is not difficult to pull out, since it is fairly shallow-rooted, if you miss little pieces of it you will soon have full-sized plants. Pull up young plants in the spring after a rainy spell when the ground is soft, and mow any remaining plants before they go to seed.

Angelica atropurpurea (purple-stemmed angelica) is native to the central and northeastern United States and adjoining Canadian provinces. This weedy, biennial angelica grows in rich soils in roadsides, neglected pastures, and waste areas. The main stem is thick and sturdy, growing above a stout, thick, branched taproot. You can easily get rid of first-year plants by hoeing out the rosettes. Mow second-season plants before they go to seed.

Anthriscus sylvestris (cow parsley) is a native of Asia, Europe, and Africa that came to the United States in wildflower mixes. It is considered a noxious weed in northeastern and northwestern North America, where it competes too successfully with pasture and hay crops. Further, it is a threat to crops such as carrots, parsnips, and celery, as it is a host for viruses such as the parsnip yellow fleck virus.

Carum carvi (caraway) is a perennial culinary herb that was brought to North America from its native Eurasia by early settlers. It has escaped from American gardens and naturalized through much of the northern United States, where it is now often considered a weed. Fortunately, it is easily pulled or can be mowed before it sets seed.

Cicuta maculata (water hemlock; Plate 10), one of the most poisonous members of the Apiaceae, is a perennial that grows abundantly in marshy ground, wet meadows, along streams, and in similar sites throughout much of the northeastern United States and adjacent Canada. Although it grows up to 6 feet (1.8 m) tall, it is easily pulled or dug in the spring when the ground is still soft.

Conium maculatum (poison hemlock; Plate 11) is a deadly poisonous biennial that commonly grows up to 8 feet (2.4 m) tall in waste areas, roadsides, and neglected fields in the northeastern and central United States as well as in nearby Canada. To get rid of first-year plants, use a hoe or similar tool to cut the rosettes below the soil line. Mow second-year plants before they flower.

Daucus carota (Queen Anne's lace; Plate 13) is the wild form of our favorite orange vegetable, the carrot (*D. carota* var. *sativa*). It grows along roadsides and in meadows and neglected pastures. It reproduces by seeds alone and is very prolific in its favorite sites. In gardens, control is simple by not allowing the plants to go to seed. In agricultural settings, if Queen Anne's lace has taken over hay meadows, plowing is about the only way to gain control. In fact, it may be necessary to plow and plant several times so that all the seeds in the soil have a chance to germinate. Be sure to mow before the plants set seed.

Heracleum mantegazzianum (giant hogweed) is a huge biennial or perennial that originated in the mountains of southwestern Asia. Growing to a height of 15 feet (4.5 m) or more, it resembles *H. sphondylium* subsp. *montanum* but is twice as big. Because of its stature and undeniable attractiveness, giant hogweed was mistakenly introduced as an ornamental in Europe and North America, where it easily jumped garden fences to become an invasive thug. It is listed as an invasive plant in England and the United States. It grows across much of the eastern United States, ranging as far west as Indiana, and also grows in the Pacific Northwest. It is found in disturbed or uncultivated wastelands and along railroads, roads, and streams. Avoid contact with this plant, which may cause severe photodermatitis in humans, characterized by large, painful, eruptive blisters. Hoeing the young plants in the early spring is a good control. Be sure not to let this plant go to seed.

Hydrocotyle sibthorpioides (lawn pennywort) was introduced from Asia as an ornamental ground cover and has naturalized throughout much of the mid-Atlantic states westward to at least Indiana and Kentucky. It can become a pest in lawns, where it spreads enthusiastically by means of its prostrate, creeping stems, which root readily at their nodes. With its round to shield-shaped, glossy leaves and small, crowded flower umbels, this perennial doesn't look at all like the classic Apiaceae species. The best control for lawn pennywort is to systematically hoe it out of lawns, then fill in the gaps by reseeding or sodding.

Pastinaca sativa (parsnip) is another large biennial that grows in wastelands and pastures. Growing up to about 3 feet (0.9 m) tall, this strong-smelling wild plant readily reseeds. Originally from Europe and western Asia, it has naturalized in much of the northern United States and southern Canada, where it thrives in the heavy, rich soils of neglected fields. Contact with the wet leaves can cause skin irritations in some people, with symptoms similar to those caused by poison ivy. As with the weedy angelicas, the best controls are to hoe out the first-year rosettes and be sure to mow the second-year plants before they go to seed.

Sanicula canadensis (sanicle) is a biennial or perennial native of eastern North America. It grows well in shady spots, reaching 1–2 feet (0.3–0.6 m) tall. American Indians used this plant to treat snakebites and other ailments. The fruits have bristles that are hooked and loose on their stems, and these can be a nuisance, sticking to clothing and dogs' fur—a marvelous way for plants to broadcast their seeds far and wide. Though not listed in most weed books, sanicle is described by Charles Heiser in *Weeds in My Garden* as a plant that has in recent years become a well-established weed in his Indiana garden. Again, the best controls are hoeing and mowing.

Sium suave (water parsnip; Plate 34) is a perennial native that is widespread throughout much of North America. Growing up to 6 feet (1.8 m) tall, it thrives in shallow water along muddy shores as well as in marshes and damp swales of fields and meadows. To control or eradicate this plant, pull it early in the growing season when the ground is still soft. Pulling up young plants in the spring plus mowing or cutting before seeds develop will help prevent this weedy umbel from spreading. Water parsnip is thought to be poisonous to livestock. People should avoid eating it as well.

Torilis arvensis (field hedge parsley) is quite a nuisance, as you already know if you have it growing in your gardens or cultivated fields. When the prickly fruits ripen and stick to your clothes, or to your pet's fur—a very successful way to spread the seeds far and wide—you'll wish you could destroy every single plant. Growing well in sunny spots in ordinary soil, field hedge parsley has earned a place on America's list of noxious weeds.

Torilis japonica (Japanese hedge parsley; Plates 36–38) is an annual native of Asia that has adapted all too well to the United States, now growing throughout most of the country in fields, gardens, and open woods. It reaches about 3 feet (0.9 m) tall and spreads rapidly by reseeding. The freely branching plants with their umbels of white flowers may look pretty as they bloom, but you had better cut or pull them before they go to seed or you will have a slew of them next year. The fruits, with their hooked prickles, may travel long distances as they cling to clothing and animal fur. Pulling young plants is the best control.

CHAPTER 6

Pests and Diseases

S A GARDENER I subscribe to the Plant Health Care (PHC) theory, which recommends concentrating on growing healthy plants, since healthy plants have few problems. When it was developed in the 1980s, PHC was warmly received by many gardeners who were increasingly interested in using conservative methods for pest and disease control. It is a preventive, rather than curative, approach to caring for plants and requires keeping a larger view when planning a garden.

There is a simple physiological fact at the heart of PHC: if a plant is grown in the right spot with the right conditions (soil texture, nutrients, moisture, temperature) it will be healthier and thus more resistant to pests and diseases. Knowing the origins of the plant is a good place to start. A plant from a sunny, dry region will take full sun and a well-draining soil. Likewise, a plant that comes from an area where soils are constantly moist will require similar moist conditions in the garden.

The root environment has a significant bearing on any plant's health, and so it is important to learn about the conditions of your garden soil. Visit a botanical garden or some other place where the plants you want to grow are thriving. Examine the soil, feel its texture, and even see what it smells like. Get an analytical soil test from your local extension agent, which will show you the shortcomings of your garden soil and suggest ways to amend it.

As for umbels specifically, most grow well in an average soil with a decent texture that is neither too sandy nor too clayey. Some will tolerate or even thrive under moist, even soggy or wet conditions.

Umbels are not especially fussy as to soil pH and will thrive in the same range as most garden ornamentals—somewhere between 6.5 and 7.5, slightly acid to slightly basic. In general, these plants are easy to cultivate if grown in the necessary USDA hardiness zones. (Zones and other cultivation details are given in chapter 8.)

Integrated Pest Management

PHC incorporates Integrated Pest Management (IPM) within its program. Though developed for commercial growers, IPM is equally applicable to home growing. It calls for using the safest, most conservative methods to control pests. Note that I said control, not destroy. There should be no need to completely eradicate insects just because they are found within a garden. Insects far outnumber humans and undoubtedly will outlast us, so we may as well learn to live peaceably with them as much as we can. Furthermore, many insects are beneficial and, if allowed to flourish, may pretty well control any undesirables for us.

IPM consists of several steps. First, identify the pest and use what is known about its biology and natural enemies to control it. Monitor pest populations through careful observation, discern the extent of injury to plants, and establish a tolerable threshold of injury. Use cultural, biological, and mechanical methods to control unacceptable populations, and use low-toxicity pesticides only as a last resort. Finally, evaluate your results.

The specific techniques are quite simple. Handpick and squash individual pests as soon as you notice them, or spray them with a hard, fine spray of cold water. Use natural predators such as beneficial nematodes, ladybugs, or tachinid flies, or use microbial organisms such as *Bacillus thuringiensis*, which will sicken and kill pests. Plant disease-resistant varieties. Maintain healthy, fertile soil with abundant microbial life. Destroy diseased plants, and keep your garden clean and tidy.

As it turns out, umbels can play a positive role in IPM programs by attracting beneficial insects, natural enemies of common pests of crops and ornamental plants. For instance, hoverflies (including species of *Meliscaeva, Toxomerus, Sphaerophoria,* and *Scaeva,* for those of you with entomological interests) eat the pollen and nectar produced in comparatively large quantities by plants of the parsley family. Happily, they're even more fond of eating aphids.

A study made by researchers at Oregon State University in the late 1990s showed that one plant family, Apiaceae, was consistent in attracting these predatory hoverflies and thus useful in cutting down on aphid damage. The study involved plants from several plant families placed in small plots adjacent to cornfields. Researchers monitored the feeding frequencies of the predatory insects, and hoverflies visited *Coriandrum sativum* (coriander) more often than any of the other plants during the early growing season. *Foeniculum vulgare* (fennel) was among the most popular plants for hoverflies later in the season.

But why are parsley family plants so attractive to predatory insects? One theory is that beneficial insects such as hoverflies tend to be fairly small, and so they prefer the small umbellifer flowers with their good landing platforms and easy access to nectar. It's also true that the umbels of these plants are shallow and loaded with pollen and nectar. Furthermore, the flower colors, usually whites and yellows, are attractive to many insects.

In addition to hoverflies, several other beneficial insects are attracted to umbellifers. Ichneumon wasps, which lay their eggs in the larvae of caterpillars and other herbivorous insects, thus parasitizing them, are strongly attracted to *Levisticum officinale* (lovage). *Anethum graveolens* (dill) draws predatory insects such as lacewings (*Chrysoperla carnea*), whose larvae are noted for their appetites for aphids. *Foeniculum vulgare* (fennel) also attracts, among other beneficials, ladybug beetles, including several species that feed, often both as adults and larvae, on aphids, and, depending on the species, on spider mites and scale insects as well.

Now I know why I have so few pest problems where I have planted parsley family plants. A patch of coriander, dill, or fennel can host enough beneficial insects to lower the numbers of plant pests. The icing on the cake is that these herbs are lovely ornamentals that should be welcome in almost any garden. For an ornamental bed, consider *Angelica gigas* (purple parsnip), with its handsome dark purple-red umbels and tall red stems. This umbel will attract many beneficials, including lacewings, parasitic wasps, and ladybug beetles.

Pests

Though generally pest-free, the umbels are occasionally attacked by mites or insects, including various aphids, whiteflies, and leaf miners, and by a number of larvae commonly called armyworms, cutworms, cabbage loopers, and wireworms.

One interesting creature you may find on both wild and cultivated plants of the Apiaceae is the larva of the black swallowtail butterfly, *Papilio polyxenes asterius* (Plate 40). Because of its diet, it is also commonly known as the parsnip swallowtail. If you should see a splashily colored caterpillar on your dill or fennel, it is probably the offspring of those handsome dark swallowtail butterflies. The larvae are green or black and have black bands on each segment beautifully punctuated with orange spots.

When I see these caterpillars, I leave them alone—surely I have enough of the herb to please both me and the young butterflies. By the end of July, the larvae are more than 1.5 inches (3.75 cm) long and about to pupate. The reward, the adult black swallowtail, is commonly seen from about April until late fall in flower gardens and roadsides, where it searches for nectar-bearing flowers.

Diseases

Southern blight and Texas root rot are the most common diseases affecting plants of the parsley family. Given the necessary conditions to flourish, these fungal diseases will infect not only umbels but also many other plants.

Southern blight is known by many names, including southern stem blight, southern stem rot, southern wilt, and mustard seed disease. It is caused by the fungus *Sclerotium rolfsii*, which can attack more than 500 different species of temperate and tropical plants, usually the herbaceous rather than the woody types. Carrots, parsnips, and other vegetables with fleshy roots are common victims.

Ideal environmental conditions for southern blight are warm and wet, with temperatures exceeding 70°F (21°C) and intermittent rain for several days, especially where the soil is acidic and somewhat sandy. The fungus germinates, first invading the roots and crown, then moving into the stems. It is spread by infected tools, transplanted plants, flowing water, and soil that has been moved. It can live on plant material that is dead or alive and can survive over long periods as brown sclerotia that look like mustard seeds. Sclerotia are fungal bodies that consist of dense masses of branching filaments that are resistant to environmental extremes.

When a plant becomes infected with southern blight, the first visible symptoms will be dark lesions near the soil line that appear to be water-soaked. These may girdle the stem and cause the plant to die. Leaves often turn yellow and drop. Plants frequently die within a month of infection. Infestations also affect the roots below the soil surface. A cottony webbing grows on the soil and around the roots and lower parts of the stems. This turns crusty and the sclerotia begin to appear, at first a warm tan color but gradually turning dark brown and hard. These sclerotia will remain viable in the soil or garden debris for five years or more.

There are some ways to diminish the chances that your garden will be hit with southern blight. Make sure the garden soil is well draining, and always remove plant debris. Frequent cultivation around the plants may also help keep this fungus at bay. Rotate crops, planting corn or other non-susceptible plants. Overcrowding may also encourage infection, so thin plants as needed. And always remove infected plants plus the top 6 inches (15 cm) of surrounding soil.

Texas root rot, also commonly known as cotton root rot, affects the Apiaceae and thousands of other plants, including annuals, perennials, and vegetables. It can even affect fruit trees and other woody plants, although they will succumb more slowly. The culprit here is the fungus *Phymatotrichopsis omnivora*, whose species name means "omnivorous." This pathogen will eat just about anything and therefore is able to infect more organisms than most other fungal diseases.

Like most fungi, Texas root rot develops rapidly under warm weather conditions in moist to soggy soil, especially in soils that are heavy and alkaline with a pH of 7.2 and above. It is most common during hot midsummer months when temperatures exceed 80°F (27°C). A disease of the southern United States, it occurs from southern California east to Texas, Arkansas, and Louisiana.

The leaves of infected plants wilt and dry, turning bronze or yellow. Any new growth is stunted, and plants may well die within just a few days. Necrotic root lesions will have already occurred by the time you notice the leaves turning. Cottony webbing that starts out white and gradually darkens to brown will cover the soil surface and parts of the affected plants.

Brown strands of this mycelium spread some 30 feet (9 m) every year along the soil surface and underneath, killing every susceptible plant in its way. As it grows, sclerotia form along the strands. These are round at first, then bumpy, at first pale, then darkening as they age. The mycelium can grow to cover an area anywhere from a few yards to an acre or more. The mycelia enter plants through wounds and pores, killing with poisons that affect the plant even in advance of contact.

Control of Texas root rot can only be by prevention. Plant disease-resistant and winter-hardy species, including carrots, parsnips, and monocots such as grasses. Lower the soil pH and increase the organic matter in the soil through regular use of composts and manures. Many more soil microorganisms that will attack harmful fungi are found in highly organic soil. Also be sure soil is well draining.

Help prevent diseases by sterilizing tools with a dilute solution of household bleach (one part bleach to nine parts water) or by using a disinfectant wipe on the blades between cuts. Get rid of infected plants and do not put them in compost piles. Important plants may sometimes be reclaimed if the disease is caught early and the diseased roots are trimmed. Once that is done, replant the specimen in well-drained planting medium.

CHAPTER 7

Botany of Umbels

IN NORTH AMERICA ALONE, native and introduced umbels are represented by 75–94 genera and 380–440 species, the exact number depending on whom you ask. The entire family numbers somewhere between 250 and well more than 400 genera, and between 2000 and more than 3000 species, again depending on the authority.

Plant identification is always useful, but it is particularly important to be able to distinguish between members of the Apiaceae because the family includes several highly toxic, even lethal species. For this reason, the motto of Apiaceae lovers should be, "Know your umbels!"

With this in mind, I focus here on the morphology and taxonomy of these fascinating plants. Morphology is the study of the structure of an organism, in this case the plants of a specific family. The umbels tend to share certain characteristics, and this information is extremely useful both for identification purposes and for learning more about the relationships between plant genera and species.

Taxonomy is equally worthy of consideration. Students new to botany may think all the research has been done that's worth doing, but this is hardly the case. They need only take a careful look at the Apiaceae, which is in a state of flux as far as its classification is concerned. New technologies have led to new insights that are often in conflict with the older method of classifying plants by means of their morphology. There are enough taxonomic challenges in Apiaceae alone to keep several botanists busy for their entire careers.

Morphology

Plants of the Apiaceae may be annual, biennial, or perennial. In growth habit they are usually herbaceous, though some are shrubs or subshrubs, and a few grow as trees. The umbels, or umbellifers if you prefer, are common and widely distributed in both temperate and boreal (northern coniferous) regions of the world.

Many are adaptable to a wide variety of environmental conditions and so have spread far beyond their original habitats. They grow in situations that range from very wet to very dry. Many of those cultivated in North America as shrubs or small trees originated in Central and South America. There are also woody species from Africa. Some umbels are succulent, some bear essential oils, and some carry resins in their tissues.

The single most characteristic structure of the Apiaceae is the inflorescence, usually a compound umbel with an umbrella-like appearance. A compound umbel is one that bears smaller umbels, sometimes called umbellules. The number of flowers in each umbel will depend on the species. The individual flower stalks may be of different lengths so that together they can form flat-topped umbels with all the flowers at the same level.

The compound umbels of the Apiaceae are constructed much like umbrellas, with all the pedicels of the flowers in each cluster radiating from a single spot at the end of a plant stem. In turn, the stems of the flower clusters all radiate inward to a single spot at the end of a main branch of the plant—sort of an umbrella of umbrellas.

A typical umbel flower is five-parted with an inferior ovary, that is, the ovary is located below the place where the petals and sepals attach. Each fruit is called a schizocarp and is made up of two seed-like fruitlets, called mericarps, which each bear a single dry, not fleshy, seed. The mericarps are often ribbed and sometimes winged. The schizocarp remains together until the two seeds are fully ripe, at which point the schizocarp splits along prescribed lines, thus separating the mericarps. The mericarps have tubes in their walls holding the volatile oils that may also be found in lesser concentrations in other parts of the plant. It is these volatile oils that give many plants of the parsley family their aromas and flavors.

Generally, the flowers are not capable of self-pollination and self-fertilization. Instead the pollen from the anthers of one flower pollinates the pistils of others. In the case of most umbels, the male parts mature and release pollen well before the female parts are receptive, and this, of course, favors outcrossing. The flowers are usually bisexual, and peripheral flowers of the umbels sometimes have larger petals on the side away from the center of the flower cluster. This is thought to help attract pollinators. The plants are pollinated by many different insects, including not only bees but also wasps, flies, mosquitoes, and gnats. This may, at least in part, account for the broad distribution of this family's species.

Another significant characteristic of umbels is that the stems are often hollow. In such cases the internodes of the stems are in fact hollow, but the nodes, where the leaves are attached, are solid, much like bamboo. The small to large leaves may be either basal or alternately arranged along the stem, with the upper leaves sometimes nearly opposite. The leaf has a petiole—a stalk that connects the leaf blade to the stem—and the base of the petiole has a sheath that grasps the stem. Sometimes the petiole is short and the base of the blade seems to wrap around the stem. Leaf blades are often pinnately divided, but sometimes they are only ternate, and often they are more finely divided, all the way to the midrib, and appear fern-like.

Superficially, the cluster of flower heads of some plants, such as yarrow (*Achillea* species, of the sunflower family, Asteraceae or Compositae), look like umbels, but if you look closely you will see that the stems or spokes of the individual flower heads do not meet at a single place on the stem. Having the stems of the individual flowers—the pedicels—meet at a single point is the significant characteristic of the structure of the umbel inflorescence.

Taxonomy

When you know the derivation of the scientific names, it is easier to understand the relationships between plants. When we refer to an umbel (meaning either the plant itself or its distinctive flower cluster), an umbellifer (another common name for these plants), or the Umbelliferae (the older scientific name for the family), we are using words that derive from the New Latin word *umbella*, the diminutive form of *umbra*, meaning "shade." (New Latin is the Latin used in scientific nomenclature since the Renaissance.) The word *Umbelliferae* simply means "plants bearing umbrellas."

The modern alternative to the name Umbelliferae is Apiaceae, which conforms to the botanical standard calling for all family names to end in *-aceae*. According to the *International Code of Botanical Nomenclature*, however, the name Umbelliferae can still be validly used. So it appears that the *Code*, in this case, is a bit of a fence-sitter, saying in effect, "Use whichever family name you wish." Many botanists prefer the more picturesque older name, including umbel expert Mark Watson of the Royal Botanic Garden Edinburgh. Although he uses the technically correct Apiaceae in scientific treatises, he continues to talk of the Umbelliferae. So much for the specificity of science!

Both the family name Apiaceae and the genus name *Apium* derive from the classical Greek for "celery." Although the Apiaceae is often called the parsley family, it could just as well be called the celery family (or the carrot family, for that matter).

Plants of the Apiaceae remain in a state of taxonomic flux, and much more needs to be done to get the family, genera, and species sorted out and put in proper relationship to one another. For me to delve into the labyrinth of Apiaceae taxonomy is perhaps more foolish than daring, but I will nonetheless try to provide enough information to give this fascinating family some friendly edges. If your interest in plant taxonomy is about as strong as the average person's interest in, say, the nest-building habits of African bowerbirds, I would suggest skipping this section.

For over a century this plant family was comprised of three sub-families: Hydrocotyloideae, with some 42 genera and 469–490 species; Saniculoideae, with about 9 genera and 304–325 species; and Apioideae, by far the largest subfamily, with some 404 genera and as many as 2827–2936 species. This last grouping in this outdated system of classification included the familiar herbs and edibles of the family.

Molecular-level research conducted in more recent years has indicated that this old system of classification, in which plants are grouped based on gross observations of structural and anatomical features of the reproductive parts, including fruits and seeds, is inaccurate and misleading. It has become clear that the traditional relationships seen among the complex subfamilies and among the genera that constitute them were ambiguous at best.

Botanists are now comparing DNA sequences to discover the true evolutionary history of plants, thereby dramatically revising the framework for grouping species into orders and families. This, in turn, will provide tools for further interpreting the evolution of structural, anatomical, and chemical development over the millennia.

Botanists have long been aware of a close relationship between the Apiaceae and Araliaceae, which together are in the order Apiales. Araliaceae is the ginseng or aralia family, which includes, among others, *Aralia*, *Hedera helix* (ivy), *Panax ginseng* (ginseng), and *Schefflera*. What has been accomplished is a reordering of the entire Apiales so that this order now has a new system of families and subfamilies.

The modern structure of the Apiales includes the core families Apiaceae and Araliaceae as well as several other smaller plant families. Within Apiaceae are the subfamilies Apioideae, with a basic chromosome number of 11; Saniculoideae, with a basic number of 8; Azorelloideae, also probably with a basic number of 8; and Mackinlayoideae, with a basic number of 12. Azorelloideae and Mackinlayoideae represent new subfamilies of Apiaceae. Azorelloideae contains many of the plants once placed in Hydrocotyloideae but can no longer include the genus *Hydrocotyle*, which has been moved to the Araliaceae (it does get complicated, doesn't it?). The new groupings more accurately reflect the evolution and relationships of these plant groups.

More radical is the movement that has been growing for over two decades to entirely toss out the Linnaean form of classification, a system that has been in effect since the eighteenth century, in which each plant is referred to by a two-part Latin name, the genus and the species. Critics say the Linnaean system doesn't compute in today's world, that it forces botanists to classify plants in a rigidly hierarchical system that has little to do with reality. Proponents would replace it with a system of classification that is based exclusively upon evolutionary relationships rather than shared characteristics. A 2004 article in *Scientific American* by Christine Soares described one proposed solution, the PhyloCode, a system that would recognize groups of plants and animals based on clades. A clade includes organisms descended from a common ancestor, no matter how different they may look from one another. Don't hold your breath, though. It would be years before such a proposal would go into effect, and even if adopted, it would likely supplement rather than replace the Linnaean system.

CHAPTER 8

A Catalog of Umbels, from *Aciphylla* to *Zizia*

T HIS CATALOG INCLUDES the major genera, species, and hybrids of the Apiaceae. In all, I have described more than fifty genera, including the most commonly grown of the fifty-two genera listed in Mark Griffiths' *Index of Garden Plants*, plus a few less well known genera from other sources. Many of these plants possess culinary, herbal, or medicinal properties. Some are rather more interesting as curiosities. I have, of course, included a number of the most poisonous species.

Wherever possible, I have provided the meaning of both the genus and species names. A Latinized binomial may be descriptive of the plant itself or of the place where it is found. In addition, a plant is sometimes named in recognition of a person, such as the person who first found it.

In addition to providing a general description of each plant, I have included growing tips where necessary. USDA hardiness zones are provided at the end of each plant description, provided the plant is not strictly an annual.

Aciphylla

Aciphylla (bayonet plant, spear grass). The genus name is from the Greek *aci*, meaning "sharp" or "pointed," and *phylla*, meaning "leaf." This group includes about forty perennial evergreen herbs, mostly dioecious, ranging in size from small to very large. Native to Australia and New Zealand, they may look somewhat like yuccas or palms. The rosette-forming basal leaves are usually rigid and spiky with sharp, pointed tips. Leaves may be simple or compound with linear leaflets. Plants have long taproots. The large, candelabra-like flower stalks have compound umbels with flowers of white to yellowish green. These are plants for sunny sites. They will thrive in well-draining soil that is highly organic. Where they are not hardy, in cooler climates, treat bayonet plants as annuals or carry them over as container plants indoors or in a greenhouse.

Aciphylla aurea (golden Spaniard). The epithet means "gold," referring to the yellow margins and midribs of the gray-green leaves. The divided leaves are up to 28 inches (70 cm) long and sharp enough to break skin. Plants grow up to 40 inches (100 cm) tall and wide and are dioecious. Yellow flower spikes occur in summer. This species is native to New Zealand. Zone 5.

Aciphylla colensoi (Colenso's Spaniard, wild Spaniard). This species is named for William Colenso (1811–1899), an English scholar, naturalist, and printer who published a Maori translation of the New Testament. The pungent, glaucous, blue-green leaves have red midribs and are sword-shaped, finely serrate, divided, and up to 20 inches (50 cm) long, with leaflets up to 8 inches (20 cm) by 0.5 inch (1.25 cm). This plant grows to 8 feet (2.4 m) tall and 6 feet (1.8 m) wide. Summer flowers are small and yellow-green on prickly stems. Another New Zealand native. Zone 5.

Aciphylla glaucescens. The epithet alludes to the fine whitish powdery coating on the foliage. The glaucous, narrow, spine-tipped, toothed leaves are up to 3 feet (0.9 m) long and have prominent whitish midribs. The plant grows to 3 feet (0.9 m) tall and just as wide. Flowers appear in early to late summer, growing in spikes of compound umbels. Also native to New Zealand. Zone 10.

Actinotus

Actinotus (flannel flower). The genus name is from the Greek and means "with rays." This group includes about seventeen annual or perennial plants commonly called flannel flowers because of their wooliness. All are native to New Zealand and Australia.

Actinotus helianthi (flannel flower). The epithet means "resembling sunflowers." This herbaceous or shrubby plant is erect and has deeply lobed, narrow leaves that are gray-green and wooly, even velvety. Small, white flowers appear in spring to early summer, growing in clusters surrounded by petal-like bracts that give them a daisy-like appearance. The shallow-rooted, brittle plant grows up to 24 inches (60 cm) tall. It is native to New South Wales and southern Queensland. Zone 10.

Aegopodium

Aegopodium (goutweed, bishop's weed). The genus name is from the Greek *aix*, meaning "goat," and *podion*, meaning "little foot." In early times, these plants were thought to cure gout. The genus includes five perennial species native to Europe and western Asia.

Aegopodium podagraria (goutweed, ash weed, bishop's weed, ground ash, ground elder). This plant was once thought to be a cure for gout, and the epithet derives from Greek *podagra*, meaning "gout in the feet." The common name of bishop's weed refers to how often the plant is found near church ruins. Goutweed is a rhizomatous ground cover, growing to no more than 1 foot (0.3 m) tall or so. It is very invasive, having escaped gardens to spread throughout much of North America. The green, compound leaves are ovate and toothed with three to nine leaflets. Simple to compound umbels of many-rayed white flowers appear in summer, growing on stems that rise above foliage, but these should be cut off before they go to seed. 'Variegatum' has deep green leaves with splotches and margins of white. Zones 4–9.

Aethusa

Aethusa (fool's parsley). The genus name derives from the Greek *aithon*, which means "glistening" and refers to the shiny, bright foliage.

Aethusa cynapium (fool's parsley, dog poison, dog's parsley, garden hemlock, lesser hemlock). The epithet refers to an old genus. This poisonous, weedy annual is a Eurasian native now naturalized in the northeastern United States and southeastern Canada. It is found mostly on disturbed sites, where it grows up to 28 inches (70 cm) tall. Freely branched on erect stems, the leaves are bi- or tripinnate. Compound umbels up to 2 inches (5 cm) in diameter appear in early summer or fall, bearing white flowers that lack sepals.

Aletes

Aletes. The genus name appears to derive from the ancient Greek hero Alete, son of Aegisthus, who ruled Mycenae until the former ruler returned from Tauris and killed him. It is unclear, however, what attributes of these plants persuaded Linnaeus to name the genus after Alete. This small genus comprises a half dozen or so natives of the western United States. They are small, creeping plants and have smooth, leathery leaves that are pinnate or bipinnate, with leaflets that are glabrous and ovate. The small spring flowers develop into dry fruits that are somewhat winged. The plants grow in alpine habitats where they have protection from wet winter conditions.

Aletes humilis (Colorado aletes, Larimer aletes). The epithet refers to the plant's low, dwarfish growing pattern. This rare, endangered United States native is found in Colorado near Wyoming. It has thick, leathery leaves. Small umbels of bright yellow flowers appear in spring. Zone 4.

Ammi

Ammi. The genus name is the classical name used by Dioscorides. This group comprises six annual or perennial species native to Europe and Asia but now found in southeastern North America. These species occur sporadically, mostly in disturbed areas and roadsides. They grow 8–32 inches (20–80 cm) tall, the erect, branched stems holding pinnately compound or dissected leaves. The umbels, with many rays that appear in summer, are compound,

Ammi from Elizabeth Blackwell's *A Curious Herbal* (1737). Missouri Botanical Garden Sturtevant Pre-Linnaean Collection

Ammi vulgare.

1. Blüthe
2.3. Frucht
4. Saame

Gemein Ammen.

the sepals have minute teeth, and the petals are white. Contact with members of *Ammi* causes photodermatitis, and these plants are also poisonous when taken internally.

Ammi majus (bishop's weed, bullwort, false bishop's weed, greater ammi). The epithet simply means "greater." This biennial has terminal leaf segments that are lanceolate, and leaves that are deeply toothed. The fruits are more toxic than the leaves. This species is reportedly also poisonous to livestock and fowl. Zone 6.

Anethum

Anethum (dill). The genus name is from the Greek *ano*, meaning "upward," and *theo*, meaning "I run," a reference to dill's rapid growth. These annual or biennial herbs are commonly used to enhance foods.

Anethum graveolens (dill, dill seed, dill weed, pickle herb; Plates 2 and 3). This feathery annual is originally from southwestern Asia. The epithet is from the Greek and means "strong-smelling." The primary common name is derived from the old Norse *dilla*, meaning "to soothe." Dill grows 18–36 inches (45–90 cm) tall, with small, yellow flowers borne on compound umbels. The pinnate foliage is very finely divided. Once established in a garden, this plant will often faithfully reseed itself from year to year. It is easy to grow from seed and should be planted in a sunny spot when soil temperatures reach 60°F–70°F (15°C–21°C). Average garden soil will suit it just fine, but make sure to keep the soil moist until it is well established. There are a number of good cultivars that vary somewhat in appearance and taste. 'Dukat' is a vigorous grower with abundant dark green foliage. 'Fernleaf' (Plate 4) is compact and multi-branching, growing to only 18 inches (45 cm). 'Vierling', a strong-stemmed blue-green plant with large umbels, is popular in Europe as a cut flower.

Anethum from John Gerard's *The Herball* (1597)

Angelica

Angelica (Plate 1). The genus name, derived from the early Latin *herba angelica*, refers to an ancient tale in which the medicinal qualities of these herbs were revealed by an angel. This group includes some fifty species with attractive compound umbels.

Angelica acutiloba (dong dang gui, ma huang). Both common names are widely used in China and Japan. This ornamental umbel has handsome, ferny, pinnate foliage and very fragrant white flowers. Long used medicinally in Japan and China, in recent years it has

become available for ornamental gardens in North America. It grows to 30–40 inches (75–100 cm) tall. Zone 4.

Angelica archangelica (garden angelica, archangel, wild parsnip; Plate 5). The species name refers to the archangel Raphael, who according to legend revealed the supposed medicinal features of this herb. This biennial or short-lived perennial is native from Europe to central Asia and Greenland. It grows up to 7 feet (2.1 m) tall, has deeply divided foliage growing on thick, hollow stems, and bears compound umbels of small, greenish white flowers in early summer. Grow it from seeds planted as soon as they ripen, since they lose their viability fairly quickly. For the absolute best performance, grow it in sun to partial shade with moist, well-draining soil that is slightly acid and rich with organic matter. In its first year, angelica produces foliage but no stalks. In its second or sometimes third year, tall stalks, flowers, and then the fruits appear, after which the plant dies in typical biennial fashion. If you should cut back the stalks in the second year, it will send up new stalks from the roots. Zone 4.

Angelica atropurpurea (purple-stemmed angelica, alexanders, American angelica, masterwort). The epithet is from the Latin *atro*, meaning "dark," and *purpurea*, meaning "purple," a reference to the stems. This biennial is native to the central and northeastern United States and adjoining parts of Canada. It grows up to 7 feet (2.1 m) tall, with foliage that is toothed and pinnate to ternate. White flowers are in compound umbels. Though attractive, this plant is invasive and is considered a weed. Zone 4.

Angelica gigas (purple parsnip, Korean angelica). The epithet means "giant" and refers to the overall size of this plant, which is originally from Korea, China, and Japan. It is tall and vigorous, growing to 3 feet (0.9 m) tall or more and equally wide. Unlike typical angelicas, it has dark purple leaf sheaths, but the foliage is otherwise characteristic, deeply divided and much like coarse ferns. Beet-red umbels that appear in the fall are up to 4 inches (10 cm) in diameter.

Grow this plant in sun to partial shade and give it plenty of moisture. Although it can be sown in the fall and then bloom the following year, some growers prefer treating it as an annual. Zone 5.

Angelica pachycarpa (Plate 6). The epithet derives from the Greek
pachys, meaning "thick," and *carpus*, referring to the pericarp (the
wall of its black fruits). Noted for its very glossy, thick, leathery,
pinnate foliage, it bears large, compound umbels of white flowers
that have an overall tinge of pale green. The petals may be notched
or unnotched. The outer flowers have larger petals, while the inner
flowers have smaller petals all of the same size. The stems are furrowed and the plant is not aromatic. It grows to 3 feet (0.9 m) tall
and wide. Grow it in full to partial sun. From what I can gather, in
hot, dry climates such as Texas this angelica may reverse its growing cycle, becoming dormant during summer months and emerg-
ing only when cooler weather appears in the fall. Furthermore,
some plantsmen consider it a self-sowing biennial. Zone 8.

Angelica sylvestris (water squirt, wild angelica). The epithet derives from
the Latin and means "wild" or "growing in the forest." This common native of Europe has been introduced to North America. It
grows to about 36 inches (90 cm) tall. From midspring to early
summer, compound umbels bear white to pinkish flowers. The umbels are gently curved on top, neither flat nor globe-like. The foliage is fern-like and bi- to tripinnate. Zones 6–10.

Angelica venenosa (hairy angelica). The epithet means "very poisonous," fitting for a plant that can cause skin irritation, rash, and
blisters. This perennial native of the eastern United States grows to
7 feet (2.1 m) tall and has ternate, toothed leaves. The flowers are
white. Zone 4.

Anisotome

Anisotome. This name is from the Greek *anisos*, meaning "unequal,"
and *tome*, meaning "to cut," referring to the edges of the leaves. The

plants of this group, including about a dozen perennial herbs native to New Zealand, have stiff, fern-like or pinnate leaves growing from a basal crown. The large umbels have white to purplish red flowers.

Anisotome aromatica. The epithet is Latin for "aromatic" or "fragrant." Toothed leaves up to 20 inches (50 cm) long have six to twelve pairs of leaflets. This species has tough, pinnate leaves with up to twelve pairs of toothed leaflets. Zone 8.

Anthriscus

Anthriscus (chervil). The ancient Roman name of this genus derives from Latin and Greek words referring to another plant, which remains unidentified today. There are about a dozen species in this genus. Plants bear umbels of small, white flowers in the summer.

Anthriscus cerefolium (chervil). The epithet is from the Latin and means "waxy leaf." This hardy annual is originally from Europe and western Asia but now grows wild in northeastern North America from Quebec to Pennsylvania in waste places and roadsides. It reaches a height of 24 inches (60 cm) and has tripinnate leaves that are hairy underneath. The stems are hairy and furrowed. Flat-topped umbels of small, white flowers appear in early summer. This culinary herb is somewhat bitter and aromatic, with an anise-like flavor. It comes in plain and curly forms. Chervil grows best in full sun, although it will take some shade. Grow it from seed, as it will not transplant well—in fact, it is not an easy herb to grow, as it is quite delicate. If you plant the seeds in the fall, they will germinate when the weather turns warm again. You may want to plant a new crop every four weeks or so to ensure fresh chervil all season long. During the growing season, a chervil plant will grow from seedling to maturity in about eight weeks. The flowers are lovely in both fresh and dried arrangements. If you cut back the flowers be-

Anthriscus, formerly *Cerefolium*, from John Gerard's *The Herball* (1597)

fore they open, chervil will produce new foliage, a good trick for lengthening the harvest season.

Anthriscus sylvestris (cow parsley, keck). The epithet derives from the Latin for "wild" or "growing in the forest." This biennial or short-lived perennial is originally from western Asia, Europe, and northern Africa. It grows to 36 inches (90 cm) tall and has ridged or furrowed stems and tripinnate foliage. 'Ravenswing' (Plate 7) is a popular ornamental cultivar noted for its rich, deep red foliage. Grow cow parsley in full sun to partial shade. Zones 6–10.

1 *Cerefolium vulgare.*
Common Cheruill.

Apium

Apium (celery). The genus name is from the Latin word for "celery." This is the so-called type genus for the Apiaceae. This group, originally from Europe and temperate Asia, includes about twenty glabrous herbs with pinnate to ternate leaves and umbels bearing white flowers.

Apium graveolens (wild celery). This biennial has been known for thousands of years from Mediterranean countries to Asia Minor and beyond. It originally grew in marshy places, especially near the sea. There are references to it in fifth-century Chinese writings. The epithet means "heavily scented."

This plant can grow up to 3 feet (0.9 m) tall. Its pinnate leaf segments are toothed or lobed, and the stems are thick and grooved. An ornamental, biennial cultivar named 'Tricolor' has green leaves with bronze tints that are later edged with creamy white and feature a central silver stripe. Variety *dulce*, whose Latin name means "sweet," is the type of celery used in salads. It is commonly grown as an annual and has thick, overlapping leaf petioles that grow vertically and are heavily ribbed. Variety *rapaceum* (Plate 8), whose Latin name refers to turnips, is what we know as celeriac or turnip-rooted celery. It has a very thick, rotund, edible taproot and is usually grown as an annual vegetable in cool climates.

Home gardeners seldom grow these tasty umbellifers because they require a long, cool growing season of five to six months. Canada, the northern United States, and northeastern and northwestern coastal regions are good areas for growing celery in North America. These plants can also be good winter crops in southern regions of the United States. Both celery and celeriac require very rich organic soil with a pH of 6.0–7.0. Keep the soil constantly moist and sprinkle every couple of weeks with a 5-10-10 fertilizer. If you prefer, you can have nutrients released over a long period by

Apium from Elizabeth Blackwell's *A Curious Herbal* (1737). Missouri Botanical Garden Sturtevant Pre-Linnaean Collection

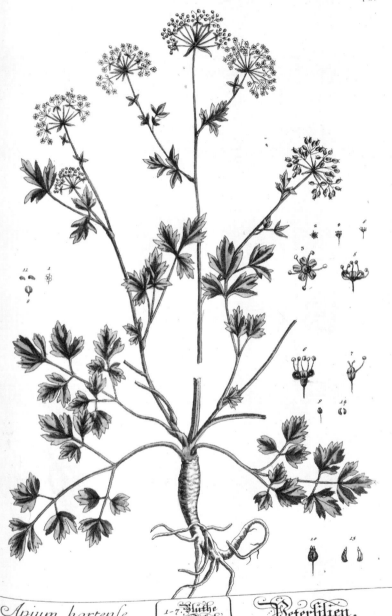

Apium hortense
Petroselinum

1–7. Blüthe
8–10. Frucht
11–13. Saame

Petersilien.

Apium.

$$\left[\begin{array}{l}1\text{-}7.\ \mathfrak{Blüthe} \\ 8.\ \mathfrak{Frucht} \\ 9\text{-}14.\ \mathfrak{Saame}\end{array}\right]$$

Sellery.

adding well-rotted cow manure to the loamy garden soil prior to each gardening season. Among the cultivars of *Apium graveolens* are both green-stalked and self-blanching types. In some areas you may be able to buy seedlings ready to plant out. If you want to grow celery from seed, plan to start about twelve weeks before transplanting into the garden. Zones 5–8.

Astrantia

Astrantia (masterwort). The genus name probably refers to the starlike umbels of these plants. Originally from Europe and Asia, this group of about ten perennial herbs has palmate or parted, glabrous leaves and simple umbels of flowers with large, showy bracts.

Astrantia major (greater masterwort). The epithet simply means "large." This native of central and eastern Europe grows to more than 30 inches (75 cm) tall and has toothed leaves with three to seven parts. The flower bracts are toothed, lanceolate, and rose or green overlaid with netting. Among the many cultivars are 'Alba', with white flowers; 'Barrister', a compact plant with white-veined leaves; 'Buckland', with domed, soft pink flowers; 'Dark Shiny Eyes', with silver centers of umbels surrounded by clear red bracts; 'Hadspen Blood', with red flowers and bracts; 'Margery Fish' (synonym 'Shaggy'), with shaggy, pinkish white flowers; 'Roma', with rich pink, unusually profuse flowers; 'Rosea', with medium pink flowers; 'Rubra', with wine-red flowers; and 'Sunningdale Variegated' (synonym 'Variegata'), with large, green leaves marked with yellow and cream and white-accented rose flowers. Zone 6.

Astrantia maxima. The epithet refers to the large size of this plant, which grows to over 36 inches (90 cm) tall. Pale pink flowers are surrounded by wide pink bracts that are pointed and sharp. This species is native to Europe and the Caucasus Mountains. The well-

Another illustration of *Apium* from *A Curious Herbal*. Missouri Botanical Garden Sturtevant Pre-Linnaean Collection

known 'Alba' has large, white bracts surrounding its small flowers. Zone 6.

Astrantia minor. The epithet refers to the small size of this astrantia, which grows to a height of only about 16 inches (40 cm). The umbel bracts are lance-shaped and usually white, though they may be tinged with red. This species is native to European mountain ranges and is well suited for alpine gardens, preferring shady, rocky sites. Zone 6.

Bupleurum

Bupleurum (thorow-wax, hare's ear). Oddly, the genus name is from the Greek *boupleuros*, meaning "ox rib," which makes to me about as much sense as the common name. This genus includes about a hundred species of annual or perennial herbs or shrubs from Europe, Asia, the northern United States, the Canary Islands, and South Africa. The leaves are entire and simple, and the compound umbels hold yellow flowers sometimes tinged with red or green. These plants are not at all fussy as to soils but grow best in full sun with good drainage.

Bupleurum falcatum (sickle-leaved hare's ear). The epithet is from the Latin, meaning "sickle-shaped." This perennial is native to Eurasia and grows to 30 inches (75 cm) tall. The glabrous basal leaves are entire, obovate, and oval, while the upper leaves are entire, lanceolate, and often curved (falcate), with prominent veining. Umbels of greenish yellow flowers appear in summer. Zone 3.

Bupleurum fruticosum (shrubby hare's ear). The epithet is from the Latin *frutex*, which means "shrub." This is an unusual parsley family member in that it is an evergreen shrub that grows to as much as 6 feet (1.8 m) tall and 8 feet (2.4 m) wide. The narrow, obovate leaves are bluish green, up to 3 inches (7.5 cm) long, and tipped with small spines that grow from the prominent midrib. Domed umbels bear bright yellow flowers during summer months. This species originated in southern Europe. Zone 7.

Bupleurum longifolium. The epithet means "long-leaved" and derives from Latin. This perennial or subshrub grow to 5 feet (1.5 m) tall. The lower leaves are elliptic and 2.4 inches (6 cm) in length. The stem leaves are more oval. Tiny, golden flowers appear in 4-inch (10 cm) umbels during summer months. Subspecies *aureum* (Plate 9) is noted for its umbels of green-centered golden flowers framed by prominent yellow bracts. *Bupleurum longifolium* is native from central Europe to Siberia. Zone 3.

Bupleurum rotundifolium (thorow-wax). The epithet means "round-leaved" and derives from Latin. This annual or short-lived perennial grows to about 24 inches (60 cm) tall. The foliage is glaucescent, meaning it has a slight bloom. The leaves are elliptic to oval, up to 2 inches (5 cm) long, and may or may not have leaf bases or petioles that clasp the stem. Greenish yellow summer flowers grow in small, pale green umbels only about 1 inch (2.5 cm) in diameter. 'Green Gold' is an attractive form with vibrant flowers. This species is native to Eurasia and the United States. Zone 6.

Carum

Carum. The genus name is the Latin version of the Greek *karon*, which refers to Caria, a region of Asia Minor where caraway was commonly grown. This genus includes about thirty species of biennial and perennial herbs from temperate to subtropical regions of Eurasia. The glabrous, compound leaves are pinnate or ternate and have narrow segments.

Carum carvi (caraway). The epithet seems to have the same derivation as that of the genus. This aromatic, flavorful, annual or biennial herb grows to 24 inches (60 cm) tall and has feathery, pinnate leaves. Summer umbels 1.5 inches (3.75 cm) in diameter bear small, white to pinkish flowers. Though it originated in Eurasia, this plant has naturalized in the United States. Caraway is hardy and easy to grow from either cuttings or seeds but is notably difficult to transplant because of its taproot. Good drainage and constantly moist soil are the keys to growing vigorous plants. Although it does best in full sun, caraway won't thrive in places with hot, humid summers like the Gulf Coast and southern Florida. Plant it in fall or early spring. Zone 3.

Chaerophyllum

Chaerophyllum. The genus name is from the Greek *chaeno*, meaning "to please," and *phyllon*, meaning "leaf," a reference to the pleasingly fragrant foliage. There are some thirty-five species in this genus of annuals, biennials, and perennials native to Eurasia and North America. The ternate or pinnately compound leaves are deeply cut, and petioles clasp the stems. Umbels of small, white flowers appear in spring.

Chaerophyllum procumbens (wild chervil). The epithet describes the plant's procumbent habit of growth. Native to the northeastern United States, this spreading, annual herb has a taproot and lanceolate basal leaves, with upper pinnate leaves that are ternately formed. Small 1-inch (2.5 cm) umbels bearing white flowers appear in spring. Wild chervil is found in many habitats, including moist forest floors. It may reach up to 15 inches (37.5 cm) tall.

Chaerophyllum tainturieri (southern chervil). The epithet is apparently not classical in origin and probably refers to the name of a person. This annual native of the southeastern United States may reach 3 feet (0.9 m) tall. Its branched stems bear leaves much like those of *C. procumbens*, and its spring umbels are also similar to that species, with small, white flowers. This plant is often found on roadsides and by railroad tracks.

Cicuta

Cicuta. The genus name is Latin and means "poison hemlock." This genus includes eight species of strong-scented perennials native to Eurasia and North America. All are poisonous, especially the roots.

Cicuta, formerly *Cicutaria*, from John Gerard's *The Herball* (1597)

Cicuta maculata (water hemlock, beaver poison, children's bane, cowbane, death of man, musquash root, snakeweed, spotted hemlock; Plate 10). The epithet is from the Latin, meaning "spotted." This plant is highly poisonous. Plants grow up to 6 feet (1.8 m) tall in wet and boggy places with sun to partial shade. The toothed leaves are bi- or tripinnate with narrow, lanceolate leaflets. Stems are thick and hollow except at the nodes. Small, white flowers grow in open, compound umbels up to 2 inches (5 cm) in diameter, appearing during summer and fall. Water hemlock has a smell similar to that of *Pastinaca sativa* (parsnip). Zone 4.

1 *Cicutaria tenuifolia.*
Thinne leafed wilde Hemlocks.

Conium

Conium. The genus name may come from the Greek *konos*, meaning "cone," referring to the umbels, or it may come from *konas*, meaning "to spin around," referring to the dizziness caused by these highly toxic plants. This genus, originally from Eurasia, includes two to three glabrous, biennial species that grow to 8 feet (2.4 m) tall or more. Compound umbels of small, white flowers appear from late spring to early summer.

Conium maculatum (poison hemlock, carrot fern, deadly hemlock, fool's parsley, hemlock, poison parsley, poison stinkweed, snakeweed, spotted hemlock, St. Bennett's weed, stinkweed, winter fern; Plate 11). The epithet means "speckled" or "spotted." This biennial, often said to be the most lethal plant in the world, is the hemlock that killed Socrates. Originally from Eurasia and northern Africa, it now grows widely throughout North America and is especially common in the Great Plains, reaching a height of about 8 feet (2.4 m). The stems are smooth and spotted with purple. The rank-smelling leaves are large, ferny, and toothed to pinnatifid, with long and spotted petioles. Large, domed, compound umbels of white flowers appear in late spring to summer. Poison hemlock has a musty smell and for this reason is sometimes called stinkweed. It has at times been confused with the tree we know as hemlock, even though the only resemblance is in the common name. Zone 5.

Coriandrum

Coriandrum. This genus includes just two annual herbs native to the Mediterranean and Asia Minor. The name is from the Greek *koriandron*, which means "bedbug," and refers to the rank smell of the unripe seeds of these plants. Leaves are pinnate with finely cut segments. Compound umbels of white to lavender flowers appear in summer to fall.

Coriandrum from Elizabeth Blackwell's *A Curious Herbal* (1737). Missouri Botanical Garden Sturtevant Pre-Linnaean Collection

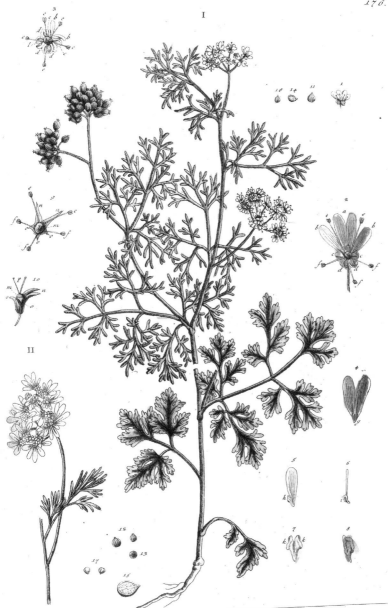

I

II

Coriandrum

{ 1–10. Blüthe
11.15. Frucht
16.17. Saame }

Coriander.

Coriandrum sativum (coriander, Chinese parsley, cilantro; Plate 12). The epithet is from the Latin *sativus*, meaning "cultivated." All parts of the plant have a strong scent. Originally from southern Europe, this widely cultivated culinary herb is an annual that grows to 20 inches (50 cm) tall. The upper leaves are pinnate to ternately pinnate and deeply cut, while the lower leaves are ovate and lobed. Small, white to pinkish to lavender flowers appear in compound umbels. Coriander is best grown from seeds, since the seedlings with their long taproots are difficult to transplant. Sow when all danger of frost is past. The plants will produce seeds by midsummer. This is another herb that will not thrive in hot, humid weather. In hotter regions it will benefit from afternoon shade.

Crithmum

Crithmum. The genus name is from the Greek *krithe*, which means "barley," a reference to the appearance of the plant's fruits. This genus has but one species.

Crithmum maritimum (samphire, sea samphire). The epithet, of course, is Latin for "sea" and refers to the plant's native habitat by the Atlantic seashores of Europe. This glabrous perennial, sometimes grown ornamentally or occasionally as a salad plant, grows up to 24 inches (60 cm) tall and has leaves that are bi- or triternate. Flat umbels of small, pale whitish yellow flowers appear in the summer. This plant, best grown from seed, thrives in sandy, gritty soils. Zone 7.

Cryptotaenia

Cryptotaenia. The first part of the genus name is from the Greek *krypto*, meaning "hidden," and the second part may refer to the bracts, which are reduced or missing. This genus includes four or five species of hairless, branching annuals or perennials. The compound leaves are ternate. Small, white flowers grow in compound umbels.

Cryptotaenia canadensis (honewort, mitsuba, white chervil). The name *canadensis* was used by early botanists to refer to plants native to

Canada and the northeastern United States, yet this perennial is also native to eastern Asia. It grows to a height of about 3 feet (0.9 m) and has smooth, serrate leaves that are three-parted, with some of the leaflets lobed. Compound umbels bear small, white flowers from May through August. Zone 4.

Cuminum

Cuminum. The genus name is the classical Greek word for this aromatic herb. The genus has two species, both annuals originally

Cuminum from John Gerard's *The Herball* (1597)

from the Mediterranean and central Asia. These plants have a thin pattern of growth, biternate leaves, and compound umbels of small, pink or white flowers.

Cuminum cyminum (cumin). The epithet, from the Latin and Greek *cyma*, may be a reference to the flower heads, in which florets in the center open first. This half-hardy annual grows to about 12 inches (30 cm) tall and has small, white to rose flowers and finely divided, feathery, deep green leaves. It is widely grown in tropical and sub-tropical regions and is another herb with a long history. Cumin requires three to four months of warm weather to mature and is unlikely to develop seeds in colder climates. The plants are fussy and will not thrive without full sun and well-draining soil. One way to grow this delicate umbel is to plant a half dozen seeds in potting medium in a pot about 4–6 inches (10–15 cm) in diameter, and then grow these indoors in bright light until night temperature are 55°F (13°C) or above. At that point, transplant the clump outdoors, taking care not to disturb the taproots.

Daucus

Daucus. The genus name is Latin for "carrot." This group includes about twenty-two annuals and biennials. Originally native from Europe to central Asia, tropical Africa, Australia, New Zealand, and the United States, these plants all have bi- or tripinnate, feathery leaves similar to carrot tops. Compound umbels bear flowers of white to pale yellow flowers.

Daucus carota (Queen Anne's lace, bird's nest, devil's plague, wild carrot; Plate 13). The epithet is a variation on the Greek *karoton*, meaning "carrot." There were many Queen Annes in European history, and it is not clear which one this plant might be named for. Some think the common name originated in England, where it applied to a

Daucus from Elizabeth Blackwell's *A Curious Herbal* (1737). Missouri Botanical Garden Sturtevant Pre-Linnaean Collection

Daucus Creticus. { 1.2. Blüthe
3. Frucht
4. Saame } Mohren-Kümmel
Cretisches Vogelnest.

wild chervil, and that somehow when the name came to America it was fastened onto the wild carrot. The name bird's nest refers to the way the flowers curl into nest-like shapes as the seeds form. Another common name is wild carrot, though this plant lacks the large and tasty root of the domesticated carrot, *D. carota* var. *sativa*. It may smell like our modern carrots, but it is tough and woody. A native of Europe, Queen Anne's lace is a biennial that grows to about 3 feet (0.9 m) tall with feathery, deeply dissected leaves that are often pinnatifid. The small flowers of the compound umbels are white to purple-tinted. The umbels are 3–4 inches (7.5–10 cm) in diameter and appear in summer to fall. They often have a single central flower of reddish purple. (According to legend, this came to be when Queen Anne pricked her finger while sewing, and a single drop of blood fell on a flower.) A curious botanist did a study of the species and discovered that only a bit more than a quarter of them have umbels with a reddish central flower. The ever-so-lacy flowers are wonderful in arrangements, whether fresh or dry. The seed heads, with their bird's nest appearance, are also good subjects for dry arrangements. Zones 3–9.

Daucus carota var. *sativa* (carrot; Plate 14). The variety name is Latin for "cultivated." This is the domestic carrot, one of the world's favorite vegetables. It has foliage similar to Queen Anne's lace but is best known for its fleshy, sweet, orange root. Though non-orange carrots are far less common, there are black, green, red, maroon, white, and yellow varieties. Home gardeners grow many types of carrots as warm-weather annuals. They grow well in temperatures of 40°F–80°F (4°C–27°C). When temperatures are higher than that, carrots do not thrive. Therefore, in regions with hot summers, carrots are best considered as spring and fall crops, or even as winter crops where temperatures seldom fall much below freezing. American gardeners grow mostly the western or carotene carrots. The other main class of carrot is known as the Asiatic carrot. It is also known as the anthocyanin carrot because its roots are usually purple. If you have light, loose, sandy soil, you can grow Imperator or

Danvers types, with their long, slender roots. If your garden soil has a lot of heavy clay or is shallow or rocky, grow the shorter Nantes or Chantenay types, which have short, thick roots or even short, rounded roots. Try studying a few seed catalogs to find carrot varieties to match your soil type. Then choose a site with at least six hours of sun. Since carrots are at their best when young, plan to sow successive crops every three to four weeks throughout the season. Zones 3–9.

Erigenia

Erigenia. The genus name is from the Greek *er* for "spring" and *genia* for "early." It is also another name for the Greek goddess of dawn, Eos (or in Roman mythology, Aurora). Both references allude to the early spring appearance of these plants. The genus *Erigenia* includes one species that is sometimes cultivated.

Erigenia bulbosa (harbinger of spring, pepper and salt; Plate 15). The epithet is Latin for "bulbous." This tuberous perennial herb, among the first plants to flower in spring, is native to the northeastern quadrant of the United States and southern Ontario. It has almost no stem, a small, round root, and bears compound umbels of white flowers with red-brown stamens. The several basal leaves are divided into narrow segments, while the upper leaves are ternate to triternate. The stems are reddish, and the leaves are a rich mid-green. This plant grows to no more than about 8 inches (20 cm) tall. Zone 3.

Eryngium

Eryngium (sea holly). The name of this genus derives from the Greek word for "thistle," which isn't surprising, since the decorative plants of this large group have flower heads that resemble thistle. There are more than 200 species of *Eryngium*, including the most widely used of the ornamental umbellifers. The leaves of this group are variously shaped and usually spiny. Stems and foliage are hairless. The flowers may be white or blue and grow in compacted umbels that do not at all resemble the usual compound umbels of most

Apiaceae. These plants are native to many parts of the world, usually inhabiting damp and marshy grasslands, coastal regions, and rocky sites. Full sun and well-draining soil are the main requirements of sea hollies.

Eryngium alpinum (alpine sea holly). The epithet is from the Latin, meaning "from high mountains." This perennial grows up to 24 inches (60 cm) tall. The blue-tinted leaves are typically spiny and triangular to cordate. Summer flowers are of a rich blue with bracts that open as pale blue, then gradually darken. Good cultivars include 'Blue Star' (Plate 16); 'Amethyst', with small, purple flowers and finely divided foliage; 'Opal', with soft lavender flowers with a silvery cast; and 'Superbum', with blue-green leaves and large, dark blue flowers. This species is native to Europe. Zone 5.

Eryngium amethystinum (amethyst sea holly; Plate 17). The epithet is from the Latin for "purple" or "violet." This perennial may reach a height of 28 inches (70 cm). The thick, green basal leaves are obovate, pinnate, and spiny, while the upper leaves are palmate with three lobes. Summer umbels range from steely blue to amethyst. Bracts are prominent, up to 2 inches (5 cm) long, with up to four pairs of spines each. This species is native to southeastern Europe, including the Balkans. Zone 2.

Eryngium aristulatum var. *parishii* (San Diego button celery, San Diego coyote thistle). This endangered California native has a low and spreading growth pattern and umbels of greenish flowers that grow in tight cylinders. It is annual and reproduces by seed.

Eryngium caucasicum (bluetop sea holly). This perennial usually grows to a height of about 15–24 inches (37.5–60 cm). Its spiny, toothed leaves have long petioles and are palmately ternate. The capsule-

Eryngium from Elizabeth Blackwell's *A Curious Herbal* (1737). Missouri Botanical Garden Sturtevant Pre-Linnaean Collection

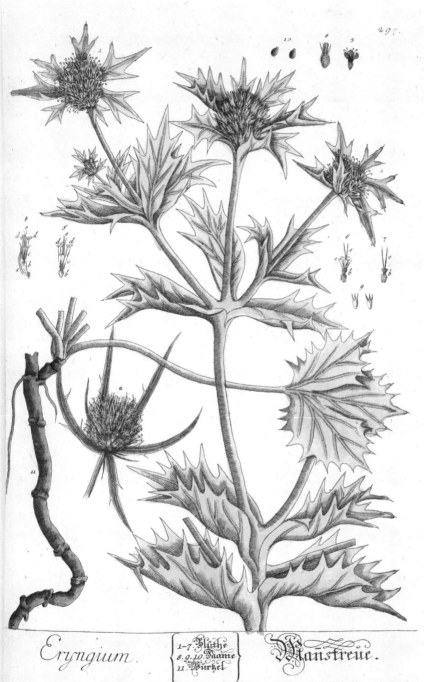

Eryngium. 1-7 Blüthe
8.9.10. Saame
11. Wurkel

Manstreüe.

like flower heads, tight umbels with spiny bracts, are of a striking blue. This species is originally from arid regions of southern Europe and western Asia, including the Caucasus, southern Russia, and northwestern Iran. While it can tolerate soil that is nutritionally poor and is not particular as to pH, this plant requires good drainage and a sunny location. A sandy soil suits it best. Zone 4.

Eryngium constancei (Constance's coyote thistle, Loch Lomond button celery, Loch Lomond coyote thistle). Named in honor of botanist Lincoln Constance, this low-growing, annual herb has spring umbels of small, white to pale purple florets. It is covered with downy, fine hairs. The slender petioles are 3–5 inches (7.5–12.5 cm) long, usually longer than the leaf blades, and have tiny spines. It reproduces by seed. An endangered United States native, it is found in the northern California counties of Lake and Sonoma.

Eryngium cuneifolium (snakeroot, wedge-leaved button snakeroot, wedge-leaved eryngo). This aromatic, perennial herb grows up to 3 feet (0.9 m) tall and features long, stalked, wedge-shaped leaves. The epithet refers to the leaves, which are odd for the Apiaceae. Several erect, branching stems up to 18 inches (45 cm) tall emerge from the basal rosette and from August to October bear small umbels of flowers with bristly bracts. The flowers are small, with white petals, filaments, styles, and stigmas accented by powdery blue anthers. This plant has a long, woody taproot and reproduces by seed. An endangered United States native, it is found only on the southern Lake Wales Ridge in Highlands County, Florida. Zone 9.

Eryngium giganteum (Miss Willmott's ghost; Plate 18). This short-lived but vigorous, rosette-forming biennial grows to 4 feet (1.2 m) tall. The basal leaves are cordate, while the stem leaves are scalloped to toothed and spiny. The cylindrical umbels, which develop in spring to early summer of the second year, are steel blue at maturity and up to 2.5 inches (6.25 cm) long, with prominent, prickly, silver-gray bracts. 'Bieberstein' is the cultivar that Ellen Willmott liked to

spread around. 'Silver Ghost' is a shorter form with gray-white flowers and narrower bracts. This species is originally from the Caucasus and Iran. Zone 6.

Eryngium leavenworthii (Leavenworth eryngo). This thistle-like annual
is native to eastern Kansas and Oklahoma, and the epithet probably
derives from the town of Leavenworth, Kansas. It grows to 40 inches
(100 cm) tall. Foliage is glabrous and purplish, with typical eryngium characteristics. Brilliant purple, cylindrical flowers grow densely, appearing from June to September. This species prefers rocky
prairies and open woodlands with limy soils. Plant it in full sun.

Eryngium variifolium (Moroccan sea holly; Plates 19 and 20). The epithet
is from the Latin *varius*, meaning "differing," and *folium*, meaning
"leaf," undoubtedly a reference to the unusual variegated leaves.
This evergreen perennial grows to about 18 inches (45 cm) tall. The
basal leaves are toothed, oblong with cordate bases, and dark green
with white marbling. The flowers appear in mid to late summer;
they are bluish gray and cylindrical with prominent grayish blue-
green bracts. This species is native to northern Africa. Zone 7.

Eryngium yuccifolium (rattlesnake master, button snakeroot; Plates 21
and 22). The epithet alludes to the spiky, yucca-like, blue-green foliage. Hairless and semi-evergreen, this perennial grows to 4 feet (1.2
m) tall. The leaves are long and thin with edges that may be either
spiny or entire. Stiff stems rise from tuberous roots; when crushed,
the stems smell like carrots. The greenish white to pale blue flowers,
appearing during summer months, are densely packed in round,
ball-like umbels about 0.5 inch (1.25 cm) or slightly more in diameter, and are surrounded by conspicuous, pointed, gray-green bracts.
This is an American native. Zone 4.

Ferula

Ferula (giant fennel). Apparently the stalks of these plants were once
used as a cane to punish school boys: the genus name is classical

Latin and means "rod used for punishment." This genus of about 170 aromatic, short-lived perennials with ferny foliage is native to a large area that stretches from the Mediterranean to central Asia. These usually glabrous plants are vigorous and grow from a thick rootstock.

Ferula assa-foetida (asafoetida, giant fennel). The epithet appears to derive from the Latin *assa*, meaning "similar to," and *foetida*, meaning "bad-smelling." This native of Iran grows to a height of 6–7 feet (1.8–2.1 m) or more. It has feathery leaves, a fleshy root, and bears flat umbels of yellow flowers during summer months. This is a tough herb, able to withstand frost. Zone 7.

Foeniculum

Foeniculum. The genus name is the classical Latin for this important herb. This genus has but one cultivated species, the plant we know as fennel. It originated in the Mediterranean.

Foeniculum vulgare (fennel; Plate 23). The epithet is Latin and means "common." This tender, aromatic annual or biennial grows up to 6 feet (1.8 m) tall and has a graceful, bushy pattern of growth. The very finely divided leaves have segments that are very narrow, and foliage ranges in color from blue-green to bronze-green. Compound umbels bear small, yellow flowers in summer months. Variety *vulgare* is the perennial fennel. Variety *azoricum* (Florence fennel, finocchio; Plate 24) is the smaller, fat-rooted annual. It grows to about 2 feet (0.6 m) tall. Variety *dulce* (sweet fennel) is the sweet annual herb. 'Smokey' (Plate 25) is a vigorous, popular cultivar. Plant fennel seeds in well-draining organic soil, either in the fall for early spring growth or in early spring. Sow every couple of weeks if you want a continuous crop. Sow Florence fennel seeds in spring or midsummer for a late fall harvest. Pinch off the flower buds to

Foeniculum from Elizabeth Blackwell's *A Curious Herbal* (1737). Missouri Botanical Garden Sturtevant Pre-Linnaean Collection

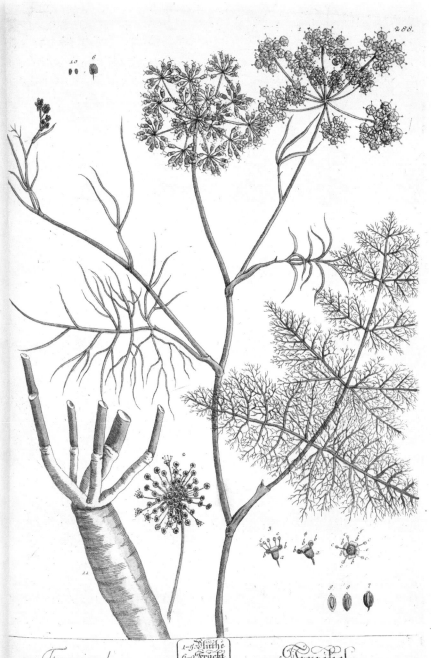

Foeniculum.

1–5. Blüthe
6–9. Frucht
10. Saame
11. Wurtzel

Fenchel.

encourage thicker stems. When Florence fennel stems are about the size of a Ping-Pong ball, cover the base of the plant to blanch it, and harvest about two weeks later. A word of warning: Don't plant fennel near *Anethum graveolens* (dill), as the two will cross-pollinate. Zone 4.

Heracleum

Heracleum (cow parsnip, giant hogweed). The genus name is a variation of the Greek *herakleia* and is a tip of the hat to the god Hercules. This group includes about sixty vigorous biennial or perennial species native to Eurasia and North America. The large, compound leaves are pinnate or ternate. The flowers of the compound umbels are white and sometimes have yellow, green, or pink overtones. These plants thrive in full sun.

Heracleum mantegazzianum (giant hogweed, cartwheel flower). The epithet honors Paolo Mantegazza (1831–1910), an Italian traveler and anthropologist. This biennial or perennial grows up to 15 feet (4.5 m) tall or more. The stems are up to 4 inches (10 cm) in diameter, ridged, hollow, and blotched with purple. The three-parted, palmate leaves are coarse and hairy, deeply lobed, and to 3 feet (0.9 m) long or more and as much as 5 feet (1.5 m) wide. Loosely compound, flat-topped umbels appear from May to July and are up to 2.5 feet (0.75 m) in diameter, with many small, white, sometimes pink-tinged, perfect flowers. Although originally imported from Asia as an ornamental, this plant has succeeded so well in Europe and North America that it is now listed as an invasive weed. Be extremely careful around this plant, as contact may result in photodermatitis. Zone 3 or 4.

Heracleum sphondylium subsp. *montanum* (cow parsnip, hogweed, masterwort; synonyms *H. lanatum, H. maximum*). The species name is an old genus name. The subspecies name is thought to derive from the fact that this plant grows in mountainous areas. It is native to Europe, Asia, and North America as far north as Alaska. A biennial or perennial that grows up to 8 feet (2.4 m) tall or more, cow parsnip has leaves that are simple and palmately lobed to pinnate. The flowers are borne in compound umbels in summer and may be white to pale yellow or pale green. Direct contact with this plant may cause dermatitis. Zone 3.

Hydrocotyle

Hydrocotyle (pennywort, navelwort, water pennywort; Plate 26). These creeping perennials live in moist and wet places, growing roots at the nodes where they touch down. They are native to many parts of the world, including the Americas, Europe, Asia, Australia, and New Zealand. Plants of this genus are appreciated by water gardeners, with the exception of *H. sibthorpioides*, a weedy species. The leaves may be simple or cleft, peltate or petiolate. The small, white flowers appear in simple or whorled umbels. Although new information about the evolutionary relationships of this genus has led specialists to remove it from the Apiaceae and place it in the Araliaceae, most growers and horticulturists (not to mention botanists) still know it, grow it, and sell it as a member of the parsley family. Pennyworts thrive in locations with sun to partial shade. Grow them in water that is up to 5 inches (12.5 cm) deep or in constantly moist soil.

Hydrocotyle sibthorpioides (lawn pennywort, navelwort). The epithet is in honor of English botanist and Oxford professor Humphrey Sibthorp (1713–1797). Originally from the marshy lowlands of eastern Asia, this aromatic, creeping perennial has small, glossy, round to shield-shaped leaves and small summer umbels, each with only a few, tiny, white flowers. Because this plant may spread too successfully, experts recommend careful control when planting it. The leaves are edible, and the plant is sometimes considered a medicinal, used to treat a variety of fevers and skin conditions. Zone 6.

Levisticum

Levisticum. The genus name is thought to be a corruption of *Ligusticum*, which refers to the Italian province Liguria, where Genoa is located. The single species is *L. officinale*.

Levisticum.

1. Blüthe
2.3. Saame
4. Würtzel

Liebstöckel.

Levisticum officinale (lovage). The Latin *officinale* is applied to plants thought to have medicinal qualities. This celery-like perennial reaches a height of 5–7 feet (1.5–2.1 m) in three to four years and smells strongly like celery. The lower leaves are triangular to diamond-shaped, while the upper leaves are bi- to tripinnate and deeply toothed. Small midsummer flowers of a greenish yellow grow in large umbels. Given a site in the garden with well-draining soil and full sun, this plant will reward you with vigor. Grow it from either seeds or cuttings. Encourage bushier growth by pinching back the flower buds and regularly harvesting the tender young leaves and stalks. After two years the roots can be harvested. Zone 5.

Lilaeopsis

Lilaeopsis. The genus name appears to refer to the foliage, which is lily-like—lanceolate, long, and narrow—on a small scale. The small perennial plants of this genus often grow in dense mats in shallow waters and on wet ground.

Lilaeopsis schaffneriana var. *recurva* (cienega false rush, Huachuca water umbel, Schaffner's grasswort). This species is obviously named in honor of someone named Schaffner, but I could not place the person. The variety name is from the Latin, meaning "curved backward," and refers to the way the leaves are shaped. This herbaceous, semi-aquatic perennial grows from rhizomes that creep along streambeds and form dense mats. Small umbels growing from the rhizome nodes bear three to ten small, greenish flowers from March to October. These develop into red fruits in late fall. This plant reproduces by seed and vegetatively. An endangered North American native, it grows at elevations of 4000–6000 feet (1200–1800 m) in marshy wetlands from Arizona to Mexico. Zone 9.

Levisticum from Elizabeth Blackwell's *A Curious Herbal* (1737). Missouri Botanical Garden Sturtevant Pre-Linnaean Collection

Lomatium

Lomatium. This genus includes some seventy species of perennials that are mostly found in western North America. The plants are stemless or short-stemmed, have roots that may be thick, and often have leaves that are dissected. Small flowers of white, yellow, or purple appear in compound umbels.

Lomatium bradshawii (Bradshaw's desert parsley, Bradshaw's lomatium, Bradshaw's parsley). This endangered United States native was once common in damp meadows and patches of prairie at low elevations in western Oregon. It is glabrous and grows to 8–20 inches (20–50 cm) tall. Most of the leaves are basal and finely divided into thread-like parts. Yellow flowers with green bracts appear in April and May. The oblong 0.5-inch (1.25 cm) fruits appear about a month later. Zone 7.

Lomatium cookii (Agate Desert lomatium, Cook's lomatium). Also an endangered United States native, this umbel grows in moist meadows and vernal pools in southwestern Oregon. Its feathery leaves are inconspicuous, and the plant is easy to pass by except when it blooms in spring. The creamy yellow flowers grow in loose, compound umbels. Zone 7.

Lomatium erythrocarpum (red-fruited desert parsley, red-fruited lomatium). This tiny plant is yet another endangered native of the United States, specifically the Blue Mountains of eastern Oregon. It reaches a height of only 0.8–2.8 inches (2–7 cm), including the flower stalk. Flowering begins in June just before the leaves begin to emerge. The small umbels bear flowers that are usually white but may be pale purple with flecks of red-purple. The red fruits are comparatively large at 0.3 inch (0.75 cm) long. Zones 5–6.

Melanoselinum

Melanoselinum. The name is from the Greek *melas*, meaning "black," and *selinon*, meaning "parsley" or "celery." The seven shrub-like species of this group bear white to purple-tinted flowers in compound umbels.

Melanoselinum decipiens (black parsley). The epithet means "deceptive," though why it applies to this plant I haven't the foggiest notion. This biennial native of Madeira grows up to 8 feet (2.4 m) tall or more and has bi- to tripinnate, toothed leaves. The dense umbels bear fragrant flowers from spring to summer. Zone 9.

Meum

Meum (baldmoney). The name is the classical Greek word for the single perennial herb included in this genus.

Meum from John Gerard's *The Herball* (1597)

Meum.

1-5. Blüthe
6-7. Frucht
8-10. Saame
11.12. Würtzel

Bärwurk.

Meum athamanticum (baldmoney, meu, spignel). The epithet is taken from Sicily's Mount Athamas, where this plant could once be found. This aromatic perennial is native to European mountains. Its leaves grow mostly in a basal rosette. The upper, pinnate leaves are finely divided with thread-like parts. Summer flowers are pink or white, sometimes tinted with purple, and grow in compound umbels. Zone 7.

Myrrhis

Myrrhis. The genus name is the Greek word for both this fragrant herb and the small tree from which the fragrant resin called myrrh is made. The genus *Myrrhis* includes just this one aromatic species.

Myrrhis odorata (sweet cicely, anise chervil, garden myrrh, myrrh, sweet chervil, sweet fern). The epithet is from the Latin and means "fragrant." This perennial, originally from Europe, grows 2–4 feet (0.6–1.2 m) tall. The bi- to tripinnate leaves are oblong, lanceolate, and deeply toothed. White flowers grow in compound 2-inch (5 cm) umbels, appearing in early summer. Sweet cicely grows at its best in moist, organic soil where there is partial to full shade. It will not thrive in regions with hot, humid summers. Try to begin with nursery plants, as this herb is not easy to grow from seed. If you can't find plants, the easiest way to grow sweet cicely from seed is to scatter the ripe black fruits where you want them to grow and then let them follow the natural cycles of the seasons; they will germinate and begin to grow in the spring. Otherwise they require up to three months of cold storage in a refrigerator if they are to germinate. Zone 5.

Oenanthe

Oenanthe (water dropwort). The genus name is from the Greek *oinos*, meaning "wine," and *anthos*, meaning "flower," a reference to the

---

Meum from Elizabeth Blackwell's *A Curious Herbal* (1737). Missouri Botanical Garden Sturtevant Pre-Linnaean Collection

Myrrhis

{ 1. Blüthe
2. Frucht
3. Saame }

Myrrhen-Körffel.
Welſcher-Körffel.

wine-like scent of the flowers from this group. The leaves are generally pinnate and toothed, and the growth pattern is creeping. The roughly thirty perennial, moisture-loving plants in this genus are native to various countries in the northern hemisphere as well as Australia and South Africa.

Oenanthe javanica (water dropwort, water celery, water parsley; synonym *O. japonica*). The epithet suggests that this creeping, stoloniferous plant is native to Java, which indeed it is. It also grows from India to Japan and as far south as Malaysia and northern Australia. Water dropwort grows up to 6–8 inches (15–20 cm) tall, with pinnate, serrate leaves. Compound umbels of small, star-like, white flowers appear in summer. Although it grows naturally in wet, organically rich soils, water dropwort will grow in gardens that are simply constantly moist. It is easy to pot up and winter over indoors. In areas with warm climates, water dropwort may succeed too well and become invasive. It has thin, horizontal stems and is easy to grow from stem and tip cuttings. 'Flamingo' (Plate 27), with its variegated white, pink, and green foliage, is a popular cultivar. Zone 6.

Osmorhiza

Osmorhiza (sweet cicely, sweet jarvil). The genus name is from the Greek *osmi*, meaning "fragrance," and *rhizo*, meaning "root." This group of ten or eleven aromatic perennial species is native to eastern Asia and North and South America. These plants have fleshy, edible roots and three-parted compound leaves with toothed to pinnatifid segments. Compound umbels have small flowers of white or yellow.

Osmorhiza claytonii (hairy sweet cicely, sweet cicely, sweet jarvil, woolly sweet cicely). This native of eastern North America is named in honor of the great English botanist John Clayton (1686–1773), who

---

Myrrhis from Elizabeth Blackwell's *A Curious Herbal* (1737).
Missouri Botanical Garden Sturtevant Pre-Linnaean Collection

came to Virginia in 1705. Hairy sweet cicely grows up to 3 feet (0.9 m) tall. It is a hairy plant with ovate, deeply toothed leaves and compound umbels of white flowers. Zone 6.

Osmorhiza longistylis (aniseroot, smooth sweet cicely). The epithet refers to the unusual length of the flower style, and as the name aniseroot suggests, this plant has a licorice-like scent. It is sometimes known as smooth sweet cicely because it is less hairy than its close relative, *O. claytonii*. The leaves of this plant, which is native to the northeastern quadrant of the United States, are biternate and toothed but less coarsely textured than those of *O. claytonii*. Some are glabrous or pubescent. White flowers are borne in compound umbels and appear in spring and summer. Zone 6.

Oxypolis

Oxypolis. The first part of the genus name is from the Greek *oxys*, meaning "sharp," probably in reference to the sharply pointed leaves. The second part of the name may come from the Latin *politus*, meaning "polished" or "neat."

Oxypolis canbyi (Canby's cowbane, Canby's dropwort). The epithet honors American botanist William Marriott Canby (1831–1904). This endangered native of the southeastern United States grows in marshy sites. It is perennial, smells slightly like dill, and grows to a height of about 3 feet (0.9 m), with quill-like leaves. Although this plant spreads mostly asexually by its rhizomatous roots, compound clusters of small, white to red-tinted flowers occasionally appear in summer. Zone 7.

Oxypolis rigidior (cowbane, hog fennel, stiff cowbane; Plate 28). The epithet is from the Latin and means "stiff" or "rigid," probably in reference to the leaves. This plant is found in damp, marshy places and ponds of the northeastern United States. It grows to a height of 5 feet (1.5 m) and has pinnate leaves with five to nine narrow leaflets that are predominantly entire. Small, white flowers appear from summer to early fall, growing in loose, compound umbels. Be careful around this plant, as contact may cause dermatitis. The roots and leaves can also poison cattle, thus the name cowbane. Zone 5.

Pastinaca

Pastinaca. The name derives from the Latin *pastus*, meaning "food." The fourteen biennial species of this Eurasian group have thick taproots and pinnate leaves.

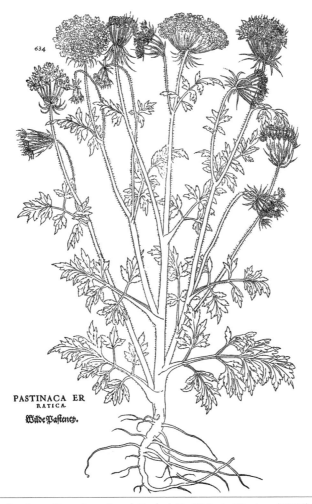

Pastinaca from Leonhard Fuchs' *De Historia Stirpium* (1542)

Pastinaca sativa (parsnip, bird's nest, hart's eye, madnip, wild parsnip). The epithet is from the Latin *sativus*, meaning "cultivated." This plant, which may grow up to 3 feet (0.9 m) tall, is cultivated as an annual for its edible root. Although originally from Europe and western Asia, it has naturalized throughout much of North America and is listed as a weed in some areas. Contact with the leaves can cause skin irritations in some people. The summer flowers are greenish yellow and grow in compound umbels. Garden parsnips, commercial descendants of the weedy original, grow best in light, moist soils that are deeply tilled and free of rocks. They thrive in soil with a pH of 5.5–7.0. Fertilize the bed with well-rotted cow manure, which releases nutrients slowly throughout the season. Or, if you prefer, use a commercial 5-10-10 fertilizer or something similar, scattering a band along both sides of the row at the rate of 5 ounces (140 g) per 10 feet (3 m) of the row. Sow the seeds thickly to make up for those that will not germinate. Sow parsnips in early spring as soon the ground thaws. Although they may be harvested in the fall, you will have sweeter parsnips if you leave them in the ground and harvest during the winter or even early spring. They are most tasty if left in the ground until you plan to use them. If your winter temperatures usually do not fall below 25°F (−4°C), you can sow parsnip seeds in early fall for harvest the following spring.

Perideridia

Perideridia. There are about nine species in this group of tuberous plants, native mostly to damp sites of the central and western United States. They have compound leaves that may be pinnate or ternate. Small flowers growing in compound umbels may be white or pink.

Perideridia americana (wild dill, eastern eulophus). The epithet, of course, identifies this perennial as an American native. It grows to a height of about 3 feet (0.9 m) tall with just a few branches growing from slender, hairless stems. The leaves are bipinnate to tripinnate and have smooth edges. Small, white flowers are in loose, compound umbels and appear from May through August. This species grows in full sun to partial shade with moist to somewhat dry soils. Zone 5.

Perideridia erythrorhiza (red-root yampah, western yampah). The epithet is from the Greek, meaning "red root." The sweet-tasting, tuberous roots of this now endangered plant were once an important part of the diet of American Indians in Oregon, where red-root yampah is native. Umbels of small, white flowers appear in summer. Zone 7.

Petroselinum

Petroselinum. The name is from the Greek *petros* for "rock" and *selinon* for "celery." This native European genus includes three biennial plants with taproots and pinnate to tripinnate leaves.

Petroselinum crispum (parsley; Plate 29). The epithet is from the Latin and means "tightly curled" in reference to the tripinnate leaves of this aromatic, biennial herb. Small, greenish yellow flowers grow in compound umbels. There are a number of cultivars, including 'Extra Curled Dwarf'; 'Green River', with bright green double-curled leaves; and 'New Dark Green', a compact dwarf with bright emerald foliage. Variety *neapolitanum* (flat-leaved parsley, Italian parsley, plain-leaved parsley; Plate 30) has flat, uncurled leaves, while variety *tuberosum* (Hamburg parsley, parsnip-rooted parsley, turnip-rooted parsley) has a thick, edible root. Parsleys are true biennials, though usually grown as annuals, developing greenish yellow flowers in their second year and then dying once the fruits have ripened. They grow to a maximum height of about 2 feet (0.6 m), usually somewhat less, and are tidy, handsome plants. In fact, they make beautiful edgings in garden beds and borders. Grow parsley in rich, well-draining soil in full sun to light shade. It will thrive if the soil is kept constantly moist but not soggy. Parsley seeds are notorious for taking a long time to germinate, up to six weeks or more, which is why many gardeners look for seedlings at their local nurseries. Once parsley begins to go to seed, its leaves become bitter, so it is best to plant it every year. Zones 7–9.

Petroselinum Macedonicum. { 1. Blüthe
2. Frucht
3.4. Saame } Macedonischer-
Peterlein.

Peucedanum

Peucedanum. The genus name is from the Greek word for "parsnip," probably a reference to the thick taproot of these plants. This genus includes about 170 perennial herbs or shrubs native to Eurasia and tropical and southern Africa. The leaves are pinnate or ternate, and the compound umbels have small flowers.

Peucedanum officinale (sulphur weed, hog fennel, sulphurwort; Plate 31). The epithet is from Latin and is applied to plants that have been used medicinally, as this plant was in the past, although it is now treated primarily as an ornamental. The name sulphur weed comes from the sulfurous odor given off by the milky sap when this plant is injured in spring. This erect, glabrous perennial will grow up to 4 feet (0.6–1.2 m) tall. The foliage is finely dissected, looking much like fennel foliage. Large, loose, compound umbels of sulfur-yellow flowers appear throughout the summer. In the wild this plant grows in salt marshes and similar habitats. It has naturalized in North America, where it may also be known as chucklusa. Zone 5.

Pimpinella

Pimpinella. The source of this name is lost in time. This is a large genus with some 150 annual and perennial species from Eurasia and northern Africa. They all have pinnate leaves and bear small, white flowers in compound umbels.

Pimpinella anisum (anise, aniseed). The epithet, of course, simply means "anise." This lanky, annual herb, which is native to Eurasia and northern Africa, grows to 2 feet (0.6 m) tall. It has simple basal leaves and upper leaves that are like those of *Petroselinum crispum* var. *neapolitanum* (flat-leaved parsley) when young, becoming more feathery as they age, like the leaves of *Anethum graveolens* (dill). Yellowish white flowers appear in summer. Grow anise from seeds

Petroselinum from Elizabeth Blackwell's *A Curious Herbal* (1737). Missouri Botanical Garden Sturtevant Pre-Linnaean Collection

planted in the spring when the soil has warmed. It will do best with full sun and average, well-draining soil.

Ptilimnium

Ptilimnium. The genus name may come from the Greek *ptilos*, meaning "feather," and *mnium*, meaning "moss." The rarity of these plants makes it difficult to discover much about the group. The leaves have delicate segments or are reduced to quill-like projections. Umbels appear in spring and have white flowers.

Ptilimnium nodosum (harperella, Piedmont mock bishopweed). The epithet is Latin and refers to the obvious nodes or joints of this plant. An endangered native of the southeastern United States, harperella grows in wet savannas and on the edges of cypress and pineland ponds and pools. It grows 6–36 inches (15–90 cm) tall. This annual species has hollow, quill-like leaves that are divided into separate chambers at the nodes. Spring umbels bear white flowers.

Sanicula

Sanicula (black snakeroot, sanicle, snakeroot). The genus name is thought to derive from the Latin *sanare*, meaning "to heal." This group includes about thirty-seven perennial or sometimes biennial species found in many parts of the world. Leaves are palmately or pinnately divided and rise directly from the ground.

Sanicula arctopoides (footsteps of spring). The epithet may derive from the Greek *arktos*, meaning "bear," though I can't find any reason for that. A native of the northwestern United States, this prostrate plant grows in clumps up to 12 inches (30 cm) in diameter and has three-parted, palmate leaves. Early summer compound umbels bear small, yellow flowers. Zone 6.

Sanicula bipinnatifida (purple sanicle). The epithet is Latin for "bipinnate," in reference to the leaflets. This plant is native from British Columbia to Baja California. It grows up to 30 inches (75 cm) tall and has purplish stems that are glabrous except at the nodes. The leaves are variable, ranging from entire to five-parted in younger plants and pinnate in older plants. Early summer flowers of yellow, purple, or red grow in compound umbels. Zone 6.

Sanicula canadensis (sanicle). The epithet refers to this plant's origins in northeastern North America. This weedy biennial or perennial grows 1–2 feet (0.3–0.6 m) tall and may be somewhat branched. The leaves are hairless, toothed, and usually trifoliate, although some of the upper leaves may be simple. White flowers appear in summer and consist of irregular, small umbels that cluster tightly in globular forms. The hooked bristles of the fruits easily grab onto fur and clothing. This plant was once used by American Indians to treat a number of conditions, including snake bite. It prefers light shade and organic soil. Zone 4.

Sanicula odorata (black snakeroot, clustered black snakeroot, clustered sanicle). The epithet refers to the fragrance associated with this plant. This perennial native of the northeastern United States is found in woodsy locations, where it grows up to 4 feet (1.2 m) tall. The compound leaves have short petioles and toothed, lanceolate leaflets. The small, pale green-yellow flowers that may appear from late spring through summer grow in sparse umbels up to 2 inches (5 cm) in diameter. Zone 6.

Selinum

Selinum. The genus name is from the Latin and means "parsley," a plant which members of this genus resemble. This group of a half dozen small to medium-sized, perennial, herbaceous plants are native from Europe to central Asia. The leaves are pinnate and triangular in their general outline. The small, purplish white to white flowers grow in umbels that have few rays.

Selinum wallichianum (milk parsley; Plate 32). The epithet honors Danish botanist Nathaniel Wallich (1786–1854), who was superintendent of the Calcutta Botanical Garden and made immense contributions to the knowledge of native Indian plants. Milk parsley is native from Pakistan and India to China, where it grows at mid to high elevations. This glabrous perennial grows up to 5 feet (1.5 m) tall and has a large taproot that is usually ridged and tinged with purple. The lacy, pinnate leaves are deeply cut and usually slightly pubescent. Stems are red. Summer flowers are white and grow in flat umbels up to 8 inches (20 cm) in diameter. Milk parsley prefers full sun to partial shade and requires a well-draining soil with a pH of 5.8–6.2. Zone 8.

Seseli

Seseli (moon carrot). This is the ancient Greek name for a genus of some sixty-five biennial or perennial herbaceous plants, native from Europe to central Asia. The leaves are pinnate to ternate. The compound umbels of flowers are usually white and appear in summer.

Seseli gummiferum (moon carrot; Plate 33). The epithet refers to the gum-like substance produced by this plant when injured. It grows to 40 inches (100 cm) tall, with fern-like leaves that are pinnatisect and finely pubescent. The foliage turns bronze-pink in fall. Compound umbels appear from summer to fall, with pale to medium pink inner flowers surrounded by whitish outer flowers. This plant is native to Crimea and the southern Aegean. It is a biennial or short-lived perennial, but since it reseeds easily, it can be kept going in garden beds. It prefers good drainage and a loamy soil. Sow the seeds in the fall for bloom the following year. Zone 5.

Sium

Sium. The genus name is from the ancient Greek *sion*, which refers to some water plants. This genus comprises about ten species of aromatic perennials that grow in wet sites.

Seseli from Elizabeth Blackwell's *A Curious Herbal* (1737). Missouri Botanical Garden Sturtevant Pre-Linnaean Collection

Seseli.

Rok Kümel
Berg-Siler.

Sium suave (water parsnip; Plate 34). The epithet is Latin for "sweet." This native of eastern Asia, the northern United States, and Canada grows to 6 feet (1.8 m) tall and has a single sturdy stem. The pinnate leaves are sparingly toothed and bear seven to seventeen linear to lanceolate leaflets. The lower leaves are often very finely divided. Small, white flowers appear in large, domed, compound umbels from summer through much of fall. Water parsnip has a fennel-like fragrance and is said to be edible, though I would definitely advise against consuming it, particularly since it is thought to be poisonous to livestock. Zone 4.

Smyrnium

Smyrnium. The genus name is from *smyrna*, the Greek word for "myrrh," and refers to the aromatic fruits and pungent smell of these plants. This group includes about seven species of smooth biennials from western Europe and the Mediterranean. The leaves are bi- or triternate.

Smyrnium olusatrum (alexander parsley, alexanders, black lovage, horse parsley, wild parsley). The epithet is from the Latin *olus*, meaning "garden herb," and *ater*, meaning "black," in reference to the black fruits of this plant. This robust biennial is glabrous, has a tuber-like root in its first year, and has a furrowed, hollow stem. The leaves are dark green, shiny, and bi- or triternate or pinnate. Native to western Europe and the Mediterranean, *S. olusatrum* has also naturalized in Bermuda. Greenish yellow spring flowers with inconspicuous calyces (the outer parts of the flowers) grow in compound umbels. Zone 9.

Smyrnium perfoliatum (perfoliate alexanders; Plate 35). The epithet is from the Latin and means "perforated leaf," a reference to the way each leaf appears to be pierced by the stem. This glabrous biennial is native to southern Europe. The bright green upper leaves are simple and ovate to cordate. The lower leaves are bi- to tripinnate or ternate. Spring or summer flowers grow in compound, greenish yellow umbels and have small sepals. Fruits are brown to black. This parsley family member is not fussy as to soil and will grow in full sun to semi-shade. A good choice for dappled shade. Zone 9.

Torilis

Torilis. The genus name is of unknown origin. The two invasive species listed here are introduced plants that have adapted all too well to American soil and climates. Both are sparingly branched and have fruits covered with bristles.

Torilis arvensis (field hedge parsley). The epithet is from the Latin and means "growing in cultivated fields." This annual grows up to 3 feet (0.9 m) tall and has bi- to tripinnate leaves. Small, white flowers appear in summer, borne in loose umbels. When ripe, the prickly fruits grab onto animals and people alike, thus traveling a good distance before dispersing the seeds.

Torilis japonica (Japanese hedge parsley; Plates 36–38). Originally from Asia, as the epithet suggests, this annual also grows to a height of about 3 feet (0.9 m) and has leaves and flowers similar to those of *T. arvensis*. The bristles on the fruits are hooked, all the better to grab onto fur or clothing. This species is far less common than *T. arvensis*, which is now a widespread noxious weed.

Trachymene

Trachymene. The genus name is from the Greek *trachys*, meaning "rough," and *meninx*, meaning "membrane," a reference to the fruits of this group. About a dozen annual, biennial, or perennial species native to Australia and the southwestern Pacific are in this genus. The leaves are usually ternately compound. White or blue flowers grow in simple umbels that appear in summer.

Trachymene coerulea (blue lace flower). The epithet is from the Latin and means "blue." This Australian annual grows up to 24 inches (60 cm) tall and has leaves that are ternate to biternate. Umbels of light blue summer flowers are up to 3 inches (7.5 cm) in diameter.

Zizia

Zizia. The genus name honors German botanist Johann Baptist Ziz (1779–1829). This genus includes four perennial North American natives, most often found growing in colonies in the dappled shade of woods. The leaves may be simple or ternately compound. Small, yellow flowers grow in umbels that appear in spring to early summer.

Zizia aptera (heart-leaved golden alexanders). The epithet is from the Latin and means "wingless." This species grows to a height of about 30 inches (75 cm) and has entire, cordate basal leaves and ternate upper leaves. From spring to early summer, small, yellow flowers appear in compound umbels. Zone 3.

Zizia aurea (golden alexanders; Plate 39). The epithet is from the Latin and means "golden," a reference to the flower color. Native from eastern Canada to the southern United States, this plant grows up to 24 inches (60 cm) tall. The compound leaves may be bi- or triternate, with lanceolate leaflets that are finely toothed. Flat-topped, compound umbels of golden flowers appear in spring to early summer. Zone 3.

Finding Information
and Plants

When searching for members of the parsley family to grow and enjoy, the first thing to do is seek out local independent nurseries that specialize in herbs and ornamental annuals, biennials, and perennials. Nursery staff are often extremely knowledgeable and can help you learn how to grow the plants well and how to find unusual species and cultivars. Such nurseries often have display gardens where you can see the plants in action. Also, there is the great advantage of not having to wait for a delivery truck—you can choose your plants and take them directly home.

Although horticulturists are bringing more and more plants, including parsley relatives, into the home marketplace, many plants remain difficult to find. The less well known umbellifers may have to be ordered by mail using catalogs that specialize in rare and unusual plants.

Botanical gardens, university extension agents, and sometimes garden clubs are good avenues for information. The Internet, of course, is also a great resource. If you don't have home access, go to your local library, where the staff can help you log on and search for information. Powerful search engines such as Google will lead you to more information than you can imagine.

Among the many associations that can help you find information and sources of plants are the Herb Society of America, North American Native Plant Society, and Perennial Plant Association. Contact information is listed on the next page.

The Herb Society of America
9019 Kirtland Chardon Road
Kirtland, Ohio 44094
United States
(440) 256-0514
www.herbsociety.org

Perennial Plant Association
3383 Schirtzinger Road
Hillard, Ohio 43026
United States
(614) 771-8431
www.perennialplant.org

**North American Native Plant
Society**
P.O. Box 84, Station D
Etobicoke, Ontario M9A 4X1
Canada
(416) 631-4438
www.nanps.org

U.S. Department of Agriculture Hardiness Zones

Average Annual Minimum Temperature

TEMPERATURE (°C)	ZONE	TEMPERATURE (°F)
Below −46	1	Below −50
−46 to −40	2	−50 to −40
−40 to −34	3	−40 to −30
−34 to −29	4	−30 to −20
−29 to −23	5	−20 to −10
−23 to −18	6	−10 to 0
−18 to −12	7	0 to 10
−12 to −7	8	10 to 20
−7 to −1	9	20 to 30
−1 to 4	10	30 to 40
Above 4	11	Above 40

Glossary

alternate: arranged singly at different points along an axis, as leaves on different sides of a stem

basal: at the base or arising from the base

bipinnate: twice pinnate, with the primary leaflets further divided into secondary leaflets

bipinnatisect: twice pinnatisect, with each leaflet further divided into secondary leaflets

biternate: twice ternate, with each of the three divisions further divided into three parts

bract: a modified leaf that is usually part of an inflorescence and encloses the stem and flower bud

carpel: one part of a pistil or ovary

compound: composed of multiple similar parts united into one whole

cordate: heart-shaped

corolla: the inner circle or second circle of the perianth or floral envelope that is composed of either separate or fused petals

cultivar: a cultivated variety, either selected from existing plants or purposely bred

dioecious: having male and female reproductive organs on separate individuals

dissected: deeply divided or cut, generally applied to leaves

elliptic: oblong and widest at the middle, with narrowed to rounded ends

entire: having a continuous and unbroken margin, especially used to describe a leaf that is not notched, toothed, or scalloped in any way

epithet: the part of a taxonomic name identifying a lesser unit within the genus (as *carota* in *Daucus carota*)

erect: perpendicular to level ground or another point of attachment

evergreen: having foliage that remains green throughout more than one growing season

filament: a thread-like part or organ, especially the stalk of the stamen that bears the anther

genus (pl. genera): a taxonomic rank that falls between family and species, comprising one or more species that share distinctive characteristics

glabrous: hairless, smooth

glaucous: having a waxy or powdery coating

habit: the general appearance and characteristics of a plant

habitat: the type of locality in which a plant grows naturally

hair: an outgrowth of the plant epidermis that may be of several types according to its form, branching, and attachment

herb: a plant without aboveground woody stems, or a plant with aromatic, medicinal, or savory qualities

herbaceous: having stems and foliage that die back to the ground each year

internode: the part of a stem between nodes

lanceolate: lance-shaped, several times longer than broad, tapering to a spear-like tip

mericarp: a carpel with a single seed, one of a pair that split at maturity

node: the place on a stem or trunk where leaves, shoots, branches, or flowers attach

obovate: egg-shaped, round at both ends, broader above the middle and more narrow below the middle

opposite: arranged in pairs at a single point along an axis, as leaves on opposite sides of a stem

ovate: egg-shaped, round at both ends, elliptical

pedicel: the stalk of an individual flower

peltate: describes a leaf attached to the stem from the inner part of the leaf rather than at the margin

perfoliate: describes a leaf that surrounds the stem so that the stem seems to go through the leaf

petiolate: having a petiole

petiole: the stalk of a leaf that attaches it to the stem

pH: a measure of hydrogen-ion concentration in the soil, used to measure soil alkalinity and acidity, with 7 indicating neutrality, higher numbers indicating alkalinity, and lower numbers indicating acidity

pinnate: feather-like, with leaflets (pinnae) arranged in two rows along the axis or rachis

pinnatifid: pinnate with deep clefts, nearly to the rachis or midrib of the leaf

pinnatisect: deeply cut almost to the midrib, with divisions more narrow than pinnatifid

pistil: a female reproductive organ of a plant, usually consisting of ovary, style, and stigma

pubescent: hairy, usually meaning covered with short, fine hairs

rhizome: a ground-level or underground, specialized stem from which roots, leaves, and stems arise

serrate: saw-toothed

simple: unbranched, not compound or divided, referring to leaves or inflorescences

species: the lowest major taxonomic rank, below the level of genus

stamen: the pollen-bearing male organ of a seed-bearing plant consisting of anther and filament, sometimes reduced to anther only

stigma: the apical part of the pistil that receives pollen and usually has a texture that is different from the rest of the style

stoloniferous: having or producing stolons (trailing shoots or stems that run along the ground and take root, giving rise to plantlets at the tip or at the nodes)

style: the more or less elongated portion of the pistil between the ovary and the stigma, absent if the stigma is sessile

subshrub: a perennial with a woody base and somewhat soft stems, or a very low shrub treated as a perennial

subspecies (subsp.): a rank of taxa below species and above variety

terminal: at the tip, apical

ternate: divided into three parts, often used to describe leaves, petals, or sepals

tripinnate: three times pinnate, with the secondary leaflets further divided into smaller leaflets

tripinnatisect: three times pinnatisect, with each secondary leaflet further divided into smaller leaflets

triternate: three times ternate, with the secondary set of three divisions further divided into three parts

tuber: a short, thick, usually subterranean modified stem or branch that bears buds and is used for food storage

tuberous: having tubers

umbel: a flat or slightly concave flower cluster in which the pedicels originate from roughly the same place

variety (var.): a rank of taxa below species and subspecies

Further Reading

The following publications were helpful during the writing of this book. I have not listed resources that include general information. You may want to pursue certain aspects of the Apiaceae, and these titles may point the way. The Internet also offers wonderful research potential, but don't take the information you find there as the gospel truth without double-checking against known resources; remember that anyone can put anything on a Web page.

Armitage, Allan M. 2001. *Armitage's Manual of Annuals, Biennials, and Half-Hardy Perennials*. Portland, Oregon: Timber Press.

Armitage, Allan M. 1997. *Herbaceous Perennial Plants*. Second Edition. Champaign, Illinois: Stipes.

Bailey, Liberty Hyde. 1949. *Manual of Cultivated Plants*. Revised edition. New York: Macmillan.

Bailey, Liberty Hyde, and Ethel Zoe Bailey. 1976. *Hortus Third*. New York: Macmillan.

Blackwell, Elizabeth. 1737. *A Curious Herbal*. John Nourse, London.

Brickell, Christopher, and Judith D. Zuk, eds. 1997. *The American Horticultural Society A–Z Encyclopedia of Garden Plants*. New York: Dorling Kindersley.

Bown, Deni. 1995. *Encyclopedia of Herbs and Their Uses*. New York: Dorling Kindersley.

Brunfels, Otto. 1530. *Herbarum Vivae Eicones*. Argentorati [Strasbourg], France: Apud Joannem Schottum [Johann Schott].

Burrows, George E., and Ronald J. Tyrl. 2001. *Toxic Plants of North America*. Ames, Iowa: Iowa State University Press.

Bush-Brown, Louise, and James Bush-Brown. 1996. *America's Garden Book*. Ed. Howard S. Irwin. New York: Macmillan.

Center for Plant Conservation. 2006. National Collection of Endangered Plants. Plant profiles. http://www. centerforplantconservation.org/NC_Choice.html.

Colley, M. R., and J. M. Luna. 2000. Relative Attractiveness of Potential Beneficial Insectary Plants to Aphidophagous Hoverflies. *Environmental Entomology* 29: 1054–1059.

Dobelis, Inge N., ed. 1986. *Magic and Medicine of Plants*. Pleasantville, New York: Reader's Digest Association.

Downie, Stephen R., Deborah S. Katz-Downie, and Mark F. Watson. 2000. A Phylogeny of the Flowering Plant Family Apiaceae. *American Journal of Botany* 87: 273–292.

Fernald, Merritt Lyndon. 1950. *Gray's Manual of Botany*. Eighth edition. New York: American Book Co.

Fuchs, Leonhard. 1542. *De Historia Stirpium Commentarii Insignes*. Basileae [Basel, Switzerland]: Officina Isingriniana.

Gardner, Jo Ann. 1998. *Herbs in Bloom*. Portland, Oregon: Timber Press.

Gerard, John. 1597. *The Herball*. London: John Norton.

Gledhill, D. 1989. *The Names of Plants*. Second edition. Cambridge, England: Cambridge University Press.

Greenwood, Pippa, Andrew Halstead, A. R. Chase, and Daniel Gilrein. 2000. *Pests and Diseases*. New York: Dorling Kindersley.

Griffiths, Mark. 1994. *Index of Garden Plants*. Portland, Oregon: Timber Press.

Heiser, Charles B. 2003. *Weeds in My Garden*. Portland, Oregon: Timber Press.

Herndon-Consagra, Francesca. 2004. *The Illustrated Garden*. St. Louis, Missouri: Missouri Botanical Garden.

Heywood, V. H., ed. 1993. *Flowering Plants of the World*. New York: Oxford University Press.

Houdret, Jessica. 2003. *Practical Herb Garden*. London: Hermes House.

Hughes, Roberta L. Summer. 1980. The Language of Herbs. *The Herb Quarterly* 2 (6): 32–34.

Knowles, George Beauchamp, and Frederic Westcott. 1837. *The Floral Cabinet and Magazine of Exotic Botany.* London: William Smith.

Kurz, Don. 1999. *Ozark Wildflowers.* Helena, Montana: Falcon.

Ladd, Doug. 1995. *Tallgrass Prairie Wildflowers.* Helena, Montana: Falcon.

Le Lièvre, Audrey. 1980. *Miss Willmott of Warley Place.* London: Faber and Faber.

Levy, Juliette de Baïracli. 1976. *Herbal Handbook for Farm and Stable.* Emmaus, Pennsylvania: Rodale Press.

Lewis, Walter H., and Memory P. F. Elvin-Lewis. 1977. *Medical Botany.* New York: Wiley.

Morton, Ian, and Judith Hall. 2001. *The Avery Complete Guide to Medicines.* New York: Avery.

Muenscher, Walter Conrad. 1955. *Weeds.* Second edition. New York: Macmillan.

Newcomb, Lawrence. 1977. *Newcomb's Wildflower Guide.* Boston: Little, Brown.

Ober, Richard, ed. 1996. *The National Herb Garden Guidebook.* Springfield, Virginia: Potomac Unit, Herb Society of America.

Pimenov, Michael G., and M. V. Leonov. 1993. *The Genera of the Umbelliferae.* Royal Botanic Gardens, Kew.

Soares, Christine. 2004. What's in a Name? *Scientific American* 291 (5): 36–37.

Swenson, Allan A. 1981. *Your Biblical Garden.* Garden City, New York: Doubleday.

Tucker, Arthur O., and Thomas DeBaggio. 2000. *The Big Book of Herbs.* Loveland, Colorado: Interweave Press.

Yatskievych, Kay. 2000. *Field Guide to Indiana Wildflowers.* Bloomington, Indiana: Indiana University Press.

Index of Plant Names

Achillea, 83
Aciphylla, 47, 48, 87–88
Aciphylla aurea, 48, 88
Aciphylla colensoi, 88
Aciphylla glaucescens, 88
Actinotus, 88
Actinotus helianthi, 89
Aegopodium, 89
Aegopodium podagraria, 70, 89
Aegopodium podagraria 'Variegatum', 48, 70, 89
Aethusa, 89
Aethusa cynapium, 23, 35, 89–90
Agate Desert lomatium. See Lomatium cookii
Aletes, 90
Aletes humilis, 63–64, 90
alexander parsley. See Smyrnium olusatrum
alexanders. See Angelica atropurpurea, Smyrnium olusatrum
alpine sea holly. See Eryngium alpinum
American angelica. See Angelica atropurpurea
amethyst sea holly. See Eryngium amethystinum
Ammi, 36, 90–92
Ammi majus, 92
Anethum, 92, 93
Anethum graveolens, 28, 39, 77, 120, 136, Plates 2 and 3
Anethum graveolens 'Dukat', 92
Anethum graveolens 'Fernleaf', 92, Plate 4
Anethum graveolens 'Vierling', 92
Angelica, 37, 55, 93, Plate 1
Angelica acutiloba, 47, 48, 93–94
Angelica archangelica, 29, 39, 42, 49, 94, Plate 5
Angelica atropurpurea, 70–71, 94

Angelica gigas, 49, 78, 94–95
Angelica pachycarpa, 49, 95, Plate 6
Angelica sylvestris, 95
Angelica venenosa, 95
anise. See Pimpinella anisum
anise chervil. See Myrrhis odorata
aniseed. See Pimpinella anisum
aniseroot. See Osmorhiza longistylis
Anisotome, 95–96
Anisotome aromatica, 96
Anthriscus, 96, 97
Anthriscus cerefolium, 24, 39–40, 96–97
Anthriscus sylvestris, 71, 97
Anthriscus sylvestris 'Ravenswing', 49–50, 97, Plate 7
Apium, 37, 84, 98, 99, 100
Apium graveolens, 29, 32, 43–44, 98, 101
Apium graveolens var. dulce, 98
Apium graveolens var. rapaceum, 43–44, 98
Apium graveolens 'Tricolor', 98
Aralia, 85
archangel. See Angelica archangelica
asafoetida. See Ferula assa-foetida
ash weed. See Aegopodium podagraria
Astrantia, 47, 50, 56, 101
Astrantia major, 50, 101
Astrantia major 'Alba', 101
Astrantia major 'Barrister', 101
Astrantia major 'Buckland', 50, 101
Astrantia major 'Dark Shiny Eyes', 101
Astrantia major 'Hadspen Blood', 50, 101
Astrantia major 'Margery Fish', 50, 101
Astrantia major 'Roma', 50, 101
Astrantia major 'Rosea', 101
Astrantia major 'Rubra', 50, 101
Astrantia major 'Shaggy'. See Astrantia major 'Margery Fish'

Astrantia major 'Sunningdale Variegated',
50, 101
Astrantia major 'Variegata'. See *Astrantia
major* 'Sunningdale Variegated'
Astrantia maxima, 50, 101–102
Astrantia maxima 'Alba', 101–102
Astrantia minor, 50, 102
baldmoney. See *Meum, Meum athamanticum*
bayonet plant. See *Aciphylla*
beaver poison. See *Cicuta maculata*
bird's nest. See *Daucus carota, Pastinaca
sativa*
bishop's weed. See *Aegopodium, Aegopodium
podagraria, Ammi majus*
black-eyed Susan. See *Rudbeckia hirta*
black lovage. See *Smyrnium olusatrum*
black parsley. See *Melanoselinum decipiens*
black snakeroot. See *Sanicula, Sanicula canadensis, Sanicula odorata*
blue lace flower. See *Trachymene coerulea*
bluetop sea holly. See *Eryngium caucasicum*
Bradshaw's desert parsley. See *Lomatium
bradshawii*
Bradshaw's lomatium. See *Lomatium bradshawii*
Bradshaw's parsley. See *Lomatium bradshawii*
bullwort. See *Ammi majus*
Bupleurum, 50–51, 102
Bupleurum falcatum, 51, 102
Bupleurum fruticosum, 51, 102
Bupleurum longifolium, 103
Bupleurum longifolium subsp. *aureum*, 51,
103, Plate 9
Bupleurum rotundifolium, 51, 103
Bupleurum rotundifolium 'Green Gold', 51,
103
button snakeroot. See *Eryngium yuccifolium*
Canby's cowbane. See *Oxypolis canbyi*
Canby's dropwort. See *Oxypolis canbyi*
caraway. See *Carum carvi*
carrot. See *Daucus carota* var. *sativa*
carrot fern. See *Conium maculatum*
cartwheel flower. See *Heracleum mantegaz-
zianum*
Carum, 103
Carum carvi, 29–30, 40, 71, 103–104
celeriac. See *Apium graveolens* var. *rapaceum*
celery. See *Apium*
Chaerophyllum, 104
Chaerophyllum procumbens, 59, 104

Chaerophyllum tainturieri, 104
chervil. See *Anthriscus, Anthriscus cerefolium*
children's bane. See *Cicuta maculata*
Chinese parsley. See *Coriandrum sativum*
chucklusa. See *Peucedanum officinale*
Cicuta, 104, 105
Cicuta maculata, 23, 24, 34, 35, 58, 71, 105,
Plate 10
cienega false rush. See *Lilaeopsis schaffneriana* var. *recurva*
cilantro. See *Coriandrum sativum*
clustered black snakeroot. See *Sanicula
odorata*
clustered sanicle. See *Sanicula odorata*
Colenso's Spaniard. See *Aciphylla colensoi*
Colorado aletes. See *Aletes humilis*
Conium, 106
Conium maculatum, 20, 23, 24, 34, 35–36,
58, 71, 106, Plate 11
Constance's coyote thistle. See *Eryngium
constancei*
Cook's lomatium. See *Lomatium cookii*
coriander. See *Coriandrum sativum*
Coriandrum, 106, 107
Coriandrum sativum, 19, 23, 30, 40, 77, 108,
Plate 12
cowbane. See *Cicuta maculata, Oxypolis
rigidior*
cow parsley. See *Anthriscus sylvestris*
cow parsnip. See *Heracleum, Heracleum
sphondylium* subsp. *montanum*
Crithmum, 108
Crithmum maritimum, 108
Cryptotaenia, 108
Cryptotaenia canadensis, 59, 108–109
cumin. See *Cuminum cyminum*
Cuminum, 109–110
Cuminum cyminum, 41, 110
curly parsley. See *Petroselinum crispum* var.
crispum
Daucus, 110, 111
Daucus carota, 68, 70, 71, 110, 112
Daucus carota var. *carota*, 44, 71
Daucus carota 'Purple Dragon', 45
Daucus carota var. *sativa*, 44–46, 71, 112–
113, Plate 14
deadly hemlock. See *Conium maculatum*
death of man. See *Cicuta maculata*
devil's plague. See *Daucus carota*
dill. See *Anethum, Anethum graveolens*
dill seed. See *Anethum graveolens*

dill weed. See *Anethum graveolens*
dog poison. See *Aethusa cynapium*
dog's parsley. See *Aethusa cynapium*
dong dang gui. See *Angelica acutiloba*
eastern eulophus. See *Perideridia americana*
Erigenia, 113
Erigenia bulbosa, 11, 59–60, 113, Plate 15
Eryngium, 22, 51–52, 56, 113–114, 115
Eryngium alpinum, 52, 114
Eryngium alpinum 'Amethyst', 114
Eryngium alpinum 'Blue Star', 114
Eryngium alpinum 'Opal', 114
Eryngium alpinum 'Superbum', 114
Eryngium amethystinum, 52, 114, Plate 17
Eryngium aristulatum var. *parishii*, 64, 114
Eryngium caucasicum, 114, 116
Eryngium constancei, 64, 116
Eryngium cuneifolium, 65, 116
Eryngium giganteum, 25, Plate 18
Eryngium giganteum 'Bieberstein', 25, 116–117
Eryngium giganteum 'Silver Ghost', 52, 117
Eryngium leavenworthii, 52, 117
Eryngium variifolium, 52, 117, Plates 19 and 20
Eryngium yuccifolium, 52, 60, 117, Plates 21 and 22
false bishop's weed. See *Ammi majus*
fennel. See *Foeniculum vulgare*
Ferula, 117–118
Ferula assa-foetida, 30–31, 41, 118
Ferula silphium, 33
field hedge parsley. See *Torilis arvensis*
finocchio. See *Foeniculum vulgare* var. *azoricum*
flannel flower. See *Actinotus, Actinotus helianthi*
flat-leaved parsley. See *Petroselinum crispum* var. *neapolitanum*
Florence fennel. See *Foeniculum vulgare* var. *azoricum*
Foeniculum, 118, 119
Foeniculum vulgare, 22, 23, 31, 41, 77, 118, 120, Plate 23
Foeniculum vulgare var. *azoricum*, 41, 118
Foeniculum vulgare var. *dulce*, 41, 118
Foeniculum vulgare 'Smokey', 118
Foeniculum vulgare var. *vulgare*, 118
fool's parsley. See *Aethusa, Aethusa cynapium, Conium maculatum*
footsteps of spring. See *Sanicula arctopoides*

garden angelica. See *Angelica archangelica*
garden hemlock. See *Aethusa cynapium*
garden myrrh. See *Myrrhis odorata*
giant fennel. See *Ferula, Ferula assa-foetida*
giant hogweed. See *Heracleum, Heracleum mantegazzianum*
golden alexanders. See *Zizia aurea*
golden Spaniard. See *Aciphylla aurea*
goutweed. See *Aegopodium, Aegopodium podagraria*
greater ammi. See *Ammi majus*
greater masterwort. See *Astrantia major*
ground ash. See *Aegopodium podagraria*
ground elder. See *Aegopodium podagraria*
hairy angelica. See *Angelica venenosa*
hairy sweet cicely. See *Osmorhiza claytonii*
Hamburg parsley. See *Petroselinum crispum* var. *tuberosum*
harbinger of spring. See *Erigenia bulbosa*
hare's ear. See *Bupleurum*
harperella. See *Ptilimnium nodosum*
hart's eye. See *Pastinaca sativa*
Hattie's pincushion. See *Astrantia major, Astrantia maxima, Astrantia minor*
heart-leaved golden alexanders. See *Zizia aptera*
Hedera helix, 85
hemlock. See *Conium maculatum*
Heracleum, 36, 53, 120
Heracleum lanatum. See *Heracleum sphondylium* subsp. *montanum*
Heracleum mantegazzianum, 53, 72, 120
Heracleum maximum. See *Heracleum sphondylium* subsp. *montanum*
Heracleum sphondylium subsp. *montanum*, 31–32, 53, 72, 120–121
hog fennel. See *Oxypolis rigidior, Peucedanum officinale*
hogweed. See *Heracleum sphondylium* subsp. *montanum*
honewort. See *Cryptotaenia canadensis*
horse parsley. See *Smyrnium olusatrum*
Huachuca water umbel. See *Lilaeopsis schaffneriana* var. *recurva*
Hydrocotyle, 53, 86, 121, Plate 26
Hydrocotyle sibthorpioides, 72, 121
Italian parsley. See *Petroselinum crispum* var. *neapolitanum*
Japanese hedge parsley. See *Torilis japonica*
keck. See *Anthriscus sylvestris*
Korean angelica. See *Angelica gigas*

Larimer aletes. See *Aletes humilis*
lawn pennywort. See *Hydrocotyle sibthor-*
  pioides
Leavenworth eryngo. See *Eryngium leaven-*
  worthii
lesser hemlock. See *Aethusa cynapium*
Levisticum, 121, 122
Levisticum officinale, 32, 41–42, 77, 123
Lilaeopsis, 123
Lilaeopsis schaffneriana var. *recurva*, 65, 123
Loch Lomond button celery. See *Eryngium*
  constancei
Loch Lomond coyote thistle. See *Eryngium*
  constancei
Lomatium, 124
Lomatium bradshawii, 66, 67, 124
Lomatium cookii, 66–67, 124
Lomatium erythrocarpum, 67, 124
lovage. See *Levisticum officinale*
madnip. See *Pastinaca sativa*
ma huang. See *Angelica acutiloba*
masterwort. See *Angelica atropurpurea*,
  Astrantia, *Heracleum sphondylium* subsp.
  montanum
Melanoselinum, 124–125
Melanoselinum decipiens, 125
meu. See *Meum athamanticum*
Meum, 125, 126
Meum athamanticum, 127
milk parsley. See *Selinum wallichianum*
Miss Willmott's ghost. See *Eryngium*
  giganteum
mitsuba. See *Cryptotaenia canadensis*
moon carrot. See *Seseli*, *Seseli gummiferum*
Moroccan sea holly. See *Eryngium varii-*
  folium
musquash root. See *Cicuta maculata*
myrrh. See *Myrrhis odorata*
Myrrhis, 127, 128
Myrrhis odorata, 19, 24, 42, 53–54, 127
navelwort. See *Hydrocotyle*, *Hydrocotyle*
  sibthorpioides
Oenanthe, 54, 127, 129
Oenanthe japonica. See *Oenanthe javanica*
Oenanthe javanica, 54, 129
Oenanthe javanica 'Flamingo', 54, 129,
  Plate 27
Osmorhiza, 129
Osmorhiza claytonii, 129–130
Osmorhiza longistylis, 60, 130
Oxypolis, 130

Oxypolis canbyi, 67–68, 130
Oxypolis rigidior, 60, 130, 131
parsley. See *Petroselinum crispum*
parsnip. See *Pastinaca sativa*
parsnip-rooted parsley. See *Petroselinum*
  crispum var. *tuberosum*
Pastinaca, 131
Pastinaca sativa, 27, 46, 73, 105, 132
pennywort. See *Hydrocotyle*
pepper and salt. See *Erigenia bulbosa*
perennial fennel. See *Foeniculum vulgare*
  var. *vulgare*
perfoliate alexanders. See *Smyrnium perfo-*
  liatum
Perideridia, 132
Perideridia americana, 61, 132–133
Perideridia erythrorhiza, 68, 133
Petroselinum, 133, 134
Petroselinum crispum, 19, 21, 24, 32–33, 42,
  133, Plate 29
Petroselinum crispum var. *crispum*, 42
Petroselinum crispum 'Extra Curled Dwarf',
  133
Petroselinum crispum 'Green River', 133
Petroselinum crispum var. *neapolitanum*, 38,
  42, 133
Petroselinum crispum 'New Dark Green', 133
Petroselinum crispum var. *tuberosum*, 42, 133
Peucedanum, 135
Peucedanum officinale, 54, 135, Plate 31
pickle herb. See *Anethum graveolens*
Piedmont mock bishopweed. See *Ptilim-*
  nium nodosum
Pimpinella, 135
Pimpinella anisum, 33, 42–43, 135–136
plain-leaved parsley. See *Petroselinum*
  crispum var. *neapolitanum*
poison hemlock. See *Conium maculatum*
poison parsley. See *Conium maculatum*
poison stinkweed. See *Conium maculatum*
Ptilimnium, 136
Ptilimnium nodosum, 68–69, 136
purple dragon carrots. See *Daucus carota*
  'Purple Dragon'
purple parsnip. See *Angelica gigas*
purple sanicle. See *Sanicula bipinnatifida*
purple-stemmed angelica. See *Angelica atro-*
  purpurea
Queen Anne's lace. See *Daucus carota*
rattlesnake master. See *Eryngium yucci-*
  folium

red-fruited desert parsley. See *Lomatium erythrocarpum*
red-fruited lomatium. See *Lomatium erythrocarpum*
red-root yampah. See *Perideridia erythrorhiza*
Rudbeckia hirta, Plate 2
St. Bennett's weed. See *Conium maculatum*
samphire. See *Crithmum maritimum*
San Diego button celery. See *Eryngium aristulatum* var. *parishii*
San Diego coyote thistle. See *Eryngium aristulatum* var. *parishii*
sanicle. See *Sanicula, Sanicula canadensis*
Sanicula, 136
Sanicula arctopoides, 136
Sanicula bipinnatifida, 136–137
Sanicula canadensis, 137
Sanicula odorata, 61, 73, 137
Schaffner's grasswort. See *Lilaeopsis schaffneriana* var. *recurva*
Schefflera, 85
sea holly. See *Eryngium*
sea samphire. See *Crithmum maritimum*
Selinum, 137
Selinum wallichianum, 54, 137–138, Plate 32
Seseli, 55, 138, 139
Seseli gummiferum, 55, 138, Plate 33
shrubby hare's ear. See *Bupleurum fruticosum*
sickle-leaved hare's ear. See *Bupleurum falcatum*
Sium, 138
Sium suave, 34, 35, 37, 61, 73, 140, Plate 34
smallage. See *Apium graveolens*
smooth sweet cicely. See *Osmorhiza longistylis*
Smyrnium, 140
Smyrnium olusatrum, 140
Smyrnium perfoliatum, 55, 140–141, Plate 35
snakeroot. See *Eryngium cuneifolium, Sanicula*
snakeweed. See *Cicuta maculata, Conium maculatum*
southern chervil. See *Chaerophyllum tainturieri*
spear grass. See *Aciphylla*
spignel. See *Meum athamanticum*
spotted hemlock. See *Conium maculatum, Cicuta maculata*
stiff cowbane. See *Oxypolis rigidior*

stinkweed. See *Conium maculatum*
sulphur weed. See *Peucedanum officinale*
sulphurwort. See *Peucedanum officinale*
sweet chervil. See *Myrrhis odorata*
sweet cicely. See *Myrrhis odorata, Osmorhiza, Osmorhiza claytonii*
sweet fennel. See *Foeniculum vulgare* var. *dulce*
sweet fern. See *Myrrhis odorata*
sweet jarvil. See *Osmorhiza, Osmorhiza claytonii*
thorow-wax. See *Bupleurum, Bupleurum rotundifolium*
Torilis, 141
Torilis arvensis, 73–74, 141
Torilis japonica, 74, 141, Plates 36–38
Trachymene, 141
Trachymene coerulea, 141–142
turnip-rooted celery. See *Apium graveolens* var. *rapaceum*
turnip-rooted parsley. See *Petroselinum crispum* var. *tuberosum*
water celery. See *Oenanthe javanica*
water dropwort. See *Oenanthe, Oenanthe javanica*
water hemlock. See *Cicuta maculata*
water parsley. See *Oenanthe javanica*
water parsnip. See *Sium suave*
water pennywort. See *Hydrocotyle*
water squirt. See *Angelica sylvestris*
wedge-leaved button snakeroot. See *Eryngium cuneifolium*
wedge-leaved eryngo. See *Eryngium cuneifolium*
western yampah. See *Perideridia erythrorhiza*
white chervil. See *Cryptotaenia canadensis*
wild angelica. See *Angelica sylvestris*
wild carrot. See *Daucus carota*
wild celery. See *Apium graveolens*
wild chervil. See *Chaerophyllum procumbens*
wild dill. See *Perideridia americana*
wild parsley. See *Smyrnium olusatrum*
wild parsnip. See *Angelica archangelica, Pastinaca sativa*
wild Spaniard. See *Aciphylla colensoi*
winter fern. See *Conium maculatum*
woolly sweet cicely. See *Osmorhiza claytonii*
Zizia, 142
Zizia aptera, 142
Zizia aurea, 61, 142, Plate 39